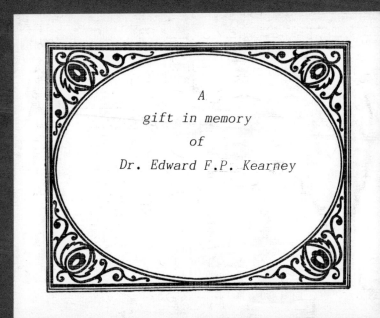

The Twisted Dream

By the Editors of Time-Life Books

Alexandria, Virginia

TIME
LIFE ®

Time-Life Books Inc.
is a wholly owned subsidiary of

The Time Inc. Book Company

President and Chief Executive Officer:
Kelso F. Sutton
President, Time Inc. Books Direct:
Christopher T. Linen

Time-Life Books Inc.

EDITOR: George Constable
Director of Design: Louis Klein
Director of Editorial Resources: Phyllis K. Wise
Director of Photography and Research:
John Conrad Weiser

PRESIDENT: John M. Fahey, Jr.
Senior Vice Presidents: Robert M. DeSena, Paul R.
Stewart, Curtis G. Viebranz, Joseph J. Ward
Vice Presidents: Stephen L. Bair, Bonita L.
Boezeman, Mary P. Donohoe, Stephen L.
Goldstein, Andrew P. Kaplan, Trevor Lunn,
Susan J. Maruyama, Robert H. Smith
New Product Development: Trevor Lunn,
Donia Ann Steele
Supervisor of Quality Control: James King

PUBLISHER: Joseph J. Ward

The Third Reich

SERIES DIRECTOR: Thomas H. Flaherty
Series Administrator: Jane Edwin
Editorial Staff for *The Twisted Dream:*
Designer: Raymond Ripper
Picture Editor: Jane Coughran
Text Editors: John Newton, Henry Woodhead
Writers: Charles J. Hagner, Stephanie A. Lewis
Researchers: Karen Monks, Trudy Pearson
(principals); Philip Brandt George,
Oobie Gleysteen
Assistant Designer: Lorraine D. Rivard
Copy Coordinator: Anne Farr
Picture Coordinator: Jennifer Iker
Editorial Assistant: Jayne A. L. Dover

Special Contributors: Ronald H. Bailey,
George Daniels, Lydia Preston Hicks, Bayard
Hooper, Thomas A. Lewis, David Nevin, Brian C.
Pohanka (text); Martha Lee Beckington
(research); Roy Nanovic (index)

Editorial Operations
Production: Celia Beattie
Library: Louise D. Forstall

Computer Composition: Deborah G. Tait
(Manager), Monika D. Thayer, Janet Barnes
Syring, Lillian Daniels

Correspondents: Elisabeth Kraemer-Singh
(Bonn), Christine Hinze (London), Christina
Lieberman (New York), Maria Vincenza Aloisi
(Paris), Ann Natanson (Rome). Valuable
assistance was also provided by: Judy Aspinall
(London); Elizabeth Brown, Katheryn White (New
York); Traudl Lessing (Vienna); Ann Wise (Rome).

Other Publications:

TIME-LIFE LIBRARY OF CURIOUS AND UNUSUAL FACTS
AMERICAN COUNTRY
VOYAGE THROUGH THE UNIVERSE
THE TIME-LIFE GARDENER'S GUIDE
MYSTERIES OF THE UNKNOWN
TIME FRAME
FIX IT YOURSELF
FITNESS, HEALTH & NUTRITION
SUCCESSFUL PARENTING
HEALTHY HOME COOKING
UNDERSTANDING COMPUTERS
LIBRARY OF NATIONS
THE ENCHANTED WORLD
THE KODAK LIBRARY OF CREATIVE PHOTOGRAPHY
GREAT MEALS IN MINUTES
THE CIVIL WAR
PLANET EARTH
COLLECTOR'S LIBRARY OF THE CIVIL WAR
THE EPIC OF FLIGHT
THE GOOD COOK
WORLD WAR II
HOME REPAIR AND IMPROVEMENT
THE OLD WEST

For information on and a full description of any
of the Time-Life Books series listed above, please
call 1-800-621-7026 or write:
Reader Information
Time-Life Customer Service
P.O. Box C-32068
Richmond, Virginia 23261-2068

The Cover: After botching a November 1923 coup
d'état in Munich, a pensive Adolf Hitler plots the
future from his Landsberg prison cell. Far from
crushing him, the time spent insulated from Germany's political turbulence allowed him to fashion
his inchoate ideas into a formidable strategy. "The
moment he is set free," warned a police report,
"Hitler will, because of his energy, again become
the driving force of new and serious public riots
and a menace to the security of the state."

This volume is one of a series that chronicles
the rise and eventual fall of Nazi Germany. Other
books in the series include:
The SS
Fists of Steel
Storming to Power
The New Order
The Reach for Empire
Lightning War
Wolf Packs
Conquest of the Balkans
Afrikakorps
The Center of the Web
Barbarossa
War on the High Seas

First printing. Printed in U.S.A.

Published simultaneously in Canada.
School and library distribution by Silver Burdett
Company, Morristown, New Jersey 07960.

TIME-LIFE is a trademark of Time Warner Inc.
U.S.A.

**Library of Congress Cataloging in
Publication Data**
The Twisted dream / by the editors of
Time-Life Books.
    p.   cm. — (The Third Reich)
    Includes bibliographical references and index.
    ISBN 0-8094-7000-4
    ISBN 0-8094-7001-2 (lib. bdg.)
    1. Germany—History—1918-1933.   2. Hitler,
Adolph, 1889-1945.   3. National socialism.
I. Time-Life Books.   II. Series.
DD237.T95 1990   943.08—dc20   90-38953

General Consultants

Col. John R. Elting, USA (Ret.), former associate professor at West Point, has written
or edited some twenty books, including
*Swords around a Throne, The Superstrate-
gists,* and *American Army Life,* as well as
Battles for Scandinavia in the Time-Life
Books World War II series. He was chief con-
sultant to the Time-Life series The Civil War.

Robert G. L. Waite is senior fellow of the
Center for Humanities and Social Sciences at
Williams College. A past senior associate
member of St. Antony's College at Oxford, he
also served for several years on the board of
the *Journal of Modern History.* Professor
Waite has written extensively on Hitler and
the rise of nazism. His books include *The
Psychopathic God: Adolf Hitler* and *Vanguard
of Nazism: The Free Corps Movement in
Postwar Germany 1918-1923.*

Contents

This allegorical painting, *The Apotheosis of Bismarck,* was commissioned in 1898 as a mourning tribute to Prince Otto von Bismarck, founder of the Second Reich. It depicts the chancellor bidding farewell to the German tribes he united as the Valkyries of Teutonic myth carry him to Valhalla, the sacred hall of fallen warriors. At left, Germania, clutching the imperial crown to her bosom, is flanked by the Prussian flag, the Hohenzollern coat of arms, and the shield of Saxony. The chained dragon at her feet represents the evils Bismarck surmounted.

Omens of a Dark Destiny

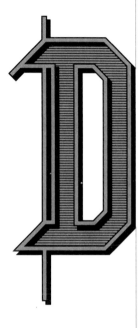

During 1834, when the fragmented German states were dominated by Prince Klemens von Metternich, chancellor of Austria, the great lyric poet Heinrich Heine penned an apocalyptic prophecy. Heine was reacting to the racist theories of his fellow nationalists, who insisted that *kultur*, a mystical spirit supposedly unique to Germans, was a more profound force than Western civilization, and that the pureblooded German people were destined to rule the earth. He foresaw a day when revolutionary forces unleashed by these doctrines would "break forth and fill the world with terror and astonishment." When that awful time arrived, the poet predicted, the "battle-madness" of the ancient Teutons would reawaken and the "demonic energies of German pantheism" would overwhelm Christianity, which had held sway over his countrymen since the year 772, when Charlemagne baptized the last of the pagan Saxon tribes.

"Should the subduing talisman, the Cross, break," Heine concluded, "then will come roaring forth the wild madness of the old champions, the insane berserker rage of which the northern poets sing. That talisman is brittle, and the day will come when it will pitifully break. The old stone gods will rise from the long-forgotten ruin and rub the dust of a thousand years from their eyes; and Thor, leaping to life with his giant hammer, will crush the Gothic cathedrals!"

Ninety-nine years later, with the advent of Adolf Hitler, Heine's nightmare came true. After gaining power in 1933, Hitler proudly proclaimed: "Yes, we are barbarians! We want to be barbarians! It is an honorable title. We shall rejuvenate the world." To Hitler, barbarism was the bedrock of all culture, the only force that could replace a dying civilization. Just as the battle-axes of the primitive German tribes had destroyed the decaying Roman Empire, so, too, would he destroy the decadent modern West. In projecting himself as a hero of German myth and Prussian military efficiency (a combination of fire and ice that Joseph Goebbels called steel romanticism), Hitler portrayed his Third Reich as part of a great historical continuum.

National socialism, the creed of Hitler and his followers, was no more inevitable in Germany than any other political ideology. But neither was it

a bizarre implant grafted onto an unreceptive nation. The Nazis themselves attributed their political success to the humiliating peace terms imposed on Germany at Versailles, by the signing of the so-called Treaty of Shame. Others, such as the German novelist Thomas Mann, winner of the Nobel Prize, reached different conclusions. From his exile in the United States in 1940, Mann declared: "Hitler, in all his wretchedness, is no accident. He could never have become possible but for certain psychological prerequisites that must be sought deeper down than in inflation, unemployment, capitalist speculation, and political intrigue."

Such remarks were often construed as anti-German warmongering in pre–Pearl Harbor America. Had not Germany enriched humankind's intellectual and spiritual heritage through the works of such native sons as Goethe and Schiller, Bach and Beethoven? But Hitler rejected Germany's humane and liberal traditions. He appealed to darker tendencies in German thought—to age-old dreams of expansion, to feelings of racial superiority, to beliefs in the supremacy of the state and the glorification of war.

The First Reich, known as the Holy Roman Empire of the German Nation, was the political entity that succeeded the empire of Charlemagne. It began in the year 962 with the coronation of Otto I, king of the Germans. Its professed goal was nothing short of the unification of all Christendom under joint temporal and ecclesiastical authority: The pope was to serve as the Vicar of Christ in spiritual affairs, and the emperor was to rule earthly matters. But things did not work out so harmoniously. While the monarchies of other European nations created dynastic nation-states, Germany remained a disunited, semifeudal backwater. Until Napoléon forcibly ended the Holy Roman Empire in 1806, a map of Germany, or more accurately, the Germanys, resembled a crazy quilt of no fewer than 314 states and 1,475 estates. Some were scarcely larger than a castle and a moat, but each had its own army, bureaucracy, currency, and court.

In the mid-twelfth century, the Reich was ruled by the emperor Frederick I, better known as Barbarossa, or Red Beard, a nickname given him by the Italians, whom he spent much time fighting. In 1190, while leading the German contingent of the Third Crusade to the Holy Land, Barbarossa, fording a stream in full armor, fell in and drowned. But according to Romantic legend, Barbarossa never died. He lives on in a secret cave high in the mountains. There he sits, deep in enchanted sleep, at a stone table guarded by his knights, his flowing beard entwined around the table and continuing to grow. Even asleep, Barbarossa remains Germany's guardian. According to one version of the tale, in Germany's greatest hour of need the ravens will awaken the warrior-king, and he will shake off the cob-

Frederick Barbarossa evoked the glories of the First Reich for generations of Germans. According to legend, he never died, but will return one day to lead Germany to a new golden age.

webs of his centuries-long slumber and come to the rescue of his people.

As the legend receded into the mists of time, it grew. In the 1890s, a marble statue of the medieval emperor was built near his supposed hiding place in the Kyffhäuser range of Thuringia. German schoolchildren, steeped in his lore, flocked to visit it. The nationalistic composer Richard Wagner looked upon him as the spiritual reincarnation of Siegfried, the legendary Nordic hero of his operatic tetralogy, *The Ring of the Nibelung*. Adolf Hitler liked to imagine that Barbarossa's cave was not in Thuringia but in his beloved Bavarian Alps near his mountain retreat at Berchtesgaden. When Nazi Germany faced its supreme military test—the invasion of the Soviet Union—that master of mass suggestion summoned the power of the ancient myth to inspire his soldiers: He changed the name of the attack plan from Fritz to Barbarossa.

Shortly after Barbarossa's death, a group of German Crusaders in Palestine founded a religious order that also became the stuff of legend—the Teutonic Knights. In return for swearing monastic vows of poverty, chastity, and obedience, each knight received a sword, a piece of bread, and an old garment. "The rules, laws, and customs of the order show us even today how highly developed was the art of dominating men and using them," wrote Heinrich von Treitschke, the immensely popular nineteenth-century Prussian historian. "In this terrible discipline, in a world that always revealed the order as grand and illustrious but the individual as insignificant and poor, there developed the spirit of selfless dedication."

In 1226, the Teutonic Knights moved to northeastern Europe near the Baltic Sea and launched a bloody crusade to Christianize the natives. After nearly exterminating them, the knights established their order as the ruling government and began repopulating the area with Germans. About three hundred years later, the order's grand master, Albert of Brandenburg, converted to Lutheranism and made the region a secular duchy. The strict code of discipline that had been part of the Teutonic Knights' religious life was transferred to service of the state. The code survived the demise of the order, forming the foundation of the Prussian officers' corps.

Martin Luther himself left behind some pernicious legacies of intolerance. Adolf Hitler regarded the towering sixteenth-century religious leader as one of his personal heroes. What appealed to Hitler was not Luther's Reformation but his chauvinism, his insistence on absolute obedience to the state, and his contempt for the Jews. The Nazis emphasized this side of Luther in a slanderous effort to turn the great churchman into one of their icons. In 1937, while attacking Lutheran ministers for not showing sufficient zeal for national socialism, the Nazi ideologue Alfred Rosenberg asserted that had Luther been alive he would have been a Party member.

Part of Rosenberg's incredible assertion was based on Luther's theory of government. Citing Rom. 13:1-6, where it is written that humankind should obey the temporal powers as the ordained of God, Luther concluded that a man could perform no greater good work than to submit to his ruler. "Those who sit in the office of magistrate, sit in the place of God," he wrote, "and their judgment is as if God judged from heaven."

Luther's mistrust of ordinary folk increased his sense of piety toward the princes. "The world and the masses are and always will be unchristian, although they are baptized and nominally Christian," he advised. "Hence a man who would venture to govern an entire community or the world with the gospel would be like a shepherd who placed in one fold wolves, lions, eagles, and sheep. The sheep would keep the peace, but they would not last long. The world cannot be ruled with a rosary."

And so he acted. When the Anabaptists, a sect practicing adult baptism, began proselytizing, Luther wanted them executed. His attitude in the Peasants' War of 1524 was equally uncharitable. When tens of thousands of serfs challenged their secular rulers, the great reformer refused to support them. "If the peasant is in open rebellion," he declared, "then he is outside the law of God. Let everyone who can, smite, slay, and stab, secretly or openly, remembering that nothing can be more poisonous, hurtful, or devilish than a rebel. It is just as when one must kill a mad dog; if you don't strike him, he will strike you."

Luther at first showed little prejudice toward Germany's Jews. He accepted their refusal to convert on the grounds that papal improprieties had ruined Christianity's appeal. His tolerance ended with his reforms. Now that the Jews had no excuse to reject the church, he called them "a plague, a pestilence, a sheer misfortune for our country." In his pamphlet entitled *On the Jews and Their Lies*, he offered advice to the German princes that the Nazis would put into practice in their *Kristallnacht* (Night of Broken Glass) pogrom of 1938: "First, set fire to their synagogues or schools; second, I advise that their houses also be razed and destroyed. This will bring home to them the fact that they are not masters in our country; third, I advise that all their prayer books and Talmudic writings be taken from them; fourth, I advise that their rabbis be forbidden to teach on pain of loss of life and limb; fifth, I advise that safe-conduct on the highways be abolished completely for the Jews, for they have no business in the countryside; sixth, I advise that usury be prohibited to them, and that all cash and treasure be taken from them; seventh, I recommend putting a flail, an ax, a spade, a distaff, or a spindle into the hands of young, strong Jews and Jewesses and letting them earn their bread in the sweat of their brow."

Unlike other European nations, which became either predominantly

Delegates ratify the Treaty of Münster, one of the pacts that ended the Thirty Years' War in 1648. The settlement recognized the sovereignty of the German states and the right of the princes to choose between Protestantism and Catholicism for themselves and their subjects.

Protestant or Catholic, the Reformation left the Germans divided between the two faiths. This religious cleavage kindled a war in 1618 when a quarrel broke out among the princes over who should be the next Holy Roman Emperor, an elected position that had been controlled by the Austrian Catholic Habsburg family since 1438. The fighting eventually involved nearly every European power. For the next thirty years, Germany was a bloody battlefield. Pillaging armies and marauding bands crisscrossed the land, laying waste to towns and villages, murdering, raping, looting, and spreading deadly epidemics of typhoid and the plague.

The agony finally ended in 1648 with the signing of treaties in the Westphalian towns of Münster and Osnabrück. The so-called Peace of Westphalia destroyed the Holy Roman Empire as a viable institution.

France came away from the negotiations with major territorial gains, including Alsace and Lorraine, and the authority to garrison the right bank of the Rhine. The German states emerged weaker and more disunited than ever. The long struggle had ravaged their lands and, by some estimates, wiped out as much as two-thirds of the population.

The German writer Hans von Grimmelshausen articulated the sentiments of many survivors through the voice of the main character in *The Adventurous Life of Simplicius Simplicissimus*, a picaresque novel based on his own childhood experiences. After his farm is sacked, Simplicissimus joins a band of marauding soldiers. He sustains himself with a dream—that one day a German hero will establish a glorious Reich. The great leader will generously permit the kings of England, Sweden, and Denmark, who are of German descent, to retain their lands as German fiefdoms, but he will wreak havoc on every other European nation. The capital of this fanciful Reich was to be a glorious new city, Germania. During the next century, a measure of the dream came true, through the efforts of the House of Hohenzollern, the royal family that united and transformed the minor states of Brandenburg and Prussia into a major European power.

Even before the final settlement of the Thirty Years' War, Frederick William of Brandenburg, known as the Great Elector for his role as one of the selectors of the Holy Roman Emperor, had lost faith in diplomacy. The only way to assure his Hohenzollern family heritage, he decided, was to create a powerful military. Within a few decades, he transformed the army from a band of ragtag mercenaries into an elite force of 30,000 men. All the while, he was also creating a bureaucracy to minister to the needs of the men in arms. To win support for his programs from the Junkers, the major landholders, who controlled the serf population, he converted their vast estates from temporary fiefdoms, granted by the crown in exchange for services, to privately owned estates, which the nobles ruled absolutely.

By the time of his death in 1688, the Great Elector had established a cult of order and discipline that would become synonymous with his native land. In 1701, his son, Frederick I, turned the Hohenzollern holdings into the kingdom of Prussia at the Baltic seaport city of Königsberg. But the Great Elector's vision of a totally militarized society did not fully take shape until his grandson, Frederick William I, assumed the throne in 1713.

This remarkable man devoted all of his considerable energies to fulfilling his grandfather's dream. Enforcing his famous dictum, "Salvation is God's affair, everything else belongs to me," Frederick William I made military service binding for all his subjects. He wrote a comprehensive set of infantry regulations that emphasized endless drill, and he made the bureaucracy even more centralized and subservient. He obligated his soldiers to swear

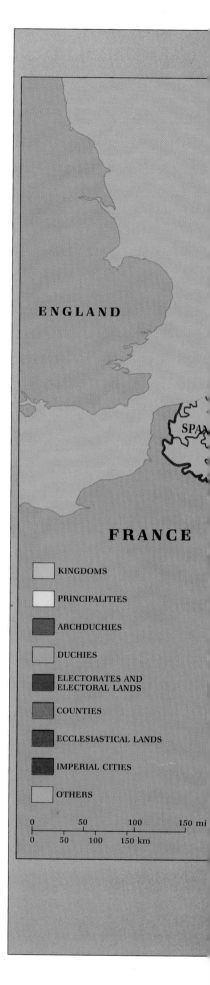

ENGLAND

SPA

FRANCE

KINGDOMS

PRINCIPALITIES

ARCHDUCHIES

DUCHIES

ELECTORATES AND
ELECTORAL LANDS

COUNTIES

ECCLESIASTICAL LANDS

IMPERIAL CITIES

OTHERS

0   50   100   150 mi

0   50   100   150 km

BALTIC
SEA

NORTH
SEA

DENMARK

HOLSTEIN

Lübeck

Hamburg

WEST POMERANIA

DUCHY
OF
PRUSSIA

BREMEN

OLDENBURG

Bremen

MECKLENBURG

LÜNEBURG

BRANDENBURG

UNITED
THERLANDS

MÜNSTER

LIPPE

MAGDEBURG

ANHALT

POLAND

MARK

WESTPHALIA

HESSE-
KASSEL

Mülhausen

SAXONY

BERG

JÜLICH

LÜTTICH

NASSAU

HESSE
DARMSTADT

THURINGIA

SILESIA

THERLANDS

TRIER

WÜRZBURG

BAYREUTH

BOHEMIA

BAMBERG

MORAVIA

PALATINATE

Rothenburg

ANSBACH

Nuremberg

METZ

Hall

BADEN

PASSAU

WÜRTTEMBERG

Ulm

BAVARIA

AUSTRIA

LOTHARINGIA

Rottweil

FRANCHE-
COMTÉ

AUGSBURG

SALZBURG

STYRIA

SWITZERLAND

TYROL

CARINTHIA

TRENT

KRAIN

SAVOY

REPUBLIC OF VENICE

PIEDMONT

ADRIATIC
SEA

HUNGARY

In the mid-seventeenth century, a map of Germany was a mosaic of many fragments. Although the Peace of Westphalia ended the devastating Thirty Years' War in 1648, the treaties meant to quell the religious and political conflicts did little to unify the various kingdoms, principalities, duchies, electorates, bishoprics, and city-states constituting the Holy Roman Empire. With the Protestant princes winning territorial sovereignty for their lands, the Catholic Habsburg emperors and the imperial diet were dubbed a "bladeless knife without a handle."

This 1901 poster commemorating the 200th anniversary of the kingdom of Prussia shows the nine monarchs of the Hohenzollern dynasty, beginning with the bewigged Frederick I *(top left)* and ending with William II *(bottom center)*. Frederick the Great, the family's most prominent member, is beneath and to the left of Frederick I.

The Hohenzollern castle, towering 1,000 feet above the South German countryside, was built during the fifteenth century in the Neckar River area of the Swabian Alps. The remains of Frederick the Great are interred within its walls.

an oath of loyalty to the institution of the kingship. "When one takes the oath to the flag one renounces oneself and surrenders entirely even one's life and everything to the monarch." Prussians called him the soldier-king; two centuries later, Oswald Spengler called him the first National Socialist.

Frederick William I recruited his officers from the Prussian aristocracy. Soon nearly every Junker family had at least one son in cadet school or in the officers' corps. The rural princes proved natural leaders of the peasant boys who made up the bulk of the ranks—the traditional lord-serf relationship simply carried over into the army.

Although Prussia ranked a mere thirteenth in Europe in terms of population, its army of 83,000 was the fourth largest on the Continent. The army budget was five times greater than that of any branch of the civil government. But for all his love of things military, Frederick William I regarded his well-trained soldiers as a purely defensive force.

Not so his gifted son, Frederick II, whose military genius earned him the title Frederick the Great. "Negotiations without weapons," he once said, "are like music without instruments." Following this credo during his forty-six-year reign, he initiated a series of wars and annexations that turned Prussia into a major Continental power.

Upon assuming the throne in 1740, Frederick II broke his father's pledge of nonaggression to the Austrian ruler Maria Theresa and launched a surprise attack on the Habsburg province of Silesia. The "Rape of Silesia" led to an eight-year war with Austria that in turn produced the Seven Years' War, a conflict pitting Prussia against a coalition of powers that included

Austria, France, Russia, Sweden, and Spain. Thanks largely to Frederick II's brilliant generalship, Prussia emerged more powerful than ever.

Frederick the Great's goal was to make the Prussian government "as coherent as a system of philosophy, so that finance, policy, and the army are coordinated to the same end: namely, the consolidation of the state and the increase of its power." Although he described himself as merely the first servant of this all-powerful state, he ruled with such an autocratic hand that his ministers were little more than filing clerks. If anything, the system worked too well; it bequeathed a legacy to future Prussians that the best government was an authoritarian one. The Junker-controlled officers' corps embodied Prussian traits. Their sense of honor and duty, harking back to the Teutonic Knights, inspired these stiff-necked aristocrats to face all manner of hardships without flinching. The French politician Honoré, comte de Mirabeau, was only half jesting when he remarked: "Prussia is not a country that has an army; it is an army that has a country."

Frederick the Great was more than a successful soldier. He was also a skilled flutist, a philosopher-poet, and a devoted patron of the arts. This unusual combination of military genius and artistic flair fascinated Adolf Hitler, who liked to think that he possessed the same qualities. During the dark days of World War II, Hitler found solace in reading about the military problems Frederick faced during the Seven Years' War. The Führer imagined that he and the great Prussian leader shared certain physical and intellectual characteristics—the same clear blue eyes, the same size hands, the same shape skull, and, of course, the same hatred of the Jews. Indeed, Hitler was so taken with the man that he bought a portrait of him and insisted on installing it wherever he resided, including his final lodging place—the subterranean Führer Bunker in Berlin.

But Frederick the Great's autocratic state did not last long without him. When he died childless in 1786, he was succeeded by his nephew Frederick William II. Shortly thereafter, the new king found himself confronted by the irrepressible forces of the French Revolution. In 1792, French armies swept across German lands, defeating both the Prussian Hohenzollerns and the Austrian Habsburgs. Frederick William II agreed to a separate peace, and for a time Prussia retained its independence. But soon it faced a more formidable opponent—Napoléon Bonaparte. In 1805, Napoléon crushed the Austrian army at Austerlitz and, a year later, defeated the Prussians at Jena. All Germany lay at the French emperor's feet.

Napoléon shattered the old order. He did away with the moribund Holy Roman Empire and, to consolidate his holdings, reduced the number of German states from more than 300 to about 30, yoking most of them to France. To balance the power of Prussia and Austria, he created a "third

Germany" out of the southern German states, including Bavaria, Württemberg, Baden, Hesse-Darmstadt, and eventually Saxony. The Rhineland was incorporated into his empire, and French troops occupied Berlin, the Prussian capital. Although many Germans grudgingly admired the modernizing reforms brought by Napoleonic rule, they resented their powerlessness. Soon German literati who were linked to the intellectual movement known as Romanticism, which had sprung from the egalitarian idealism of the French Revolution, began preaching a new gospel of nationalism. In other countries, Romanticism remained largely a literary and an artistic movement, but in Germany, it took a violent political twist.

One of the progenitors of these new ideas was the philosopher Johann Gottlieb Fichte, rector of the University of Berlin. His *Addresses to the German Nation* fired the imagination of his youthful audiences. The German people, Fichte argued, were a chosen race with a unique genius and a special right to fulfill their destiny, by force if necessary. He infused his followers with a determination to drive out the French and forge a united nation out of the separate states. Like Grimmelshausen's fictional character, he called for a great leader to create a Reich by seizing *Lebensraum*—"living space"—from Germany's neighbors.

Christian Friedrich Rühs, a history professor at the University of Berlin, shared his colleague's fanaticism. Calling the French a "villainous and odious race," he demanded that the French language be banned from schools and courts of law. Rühs especially resented the imposition of the *Code Napoléon*, for it made Jews and ethnic Germans equal before the law. Instead, he wanted to force all German Jews to wear a yellow patch so that ethnic Germans could recognize the "Hebrew enemy."

The nationalist poet Ernst Moritz Arndt was another avid Francophobe and anti-Semite. In an address delivered in 1810, he called for a "man of action," a Führer figure guided not by reason but "by the dark forces of the age, and by a darker love for his people." What Germany needed, he said, was a "military tyrant capable of exterminating whole nations."

Arndt believed that each race behaves in accordance with its historical past and that, thanks to what he imagined to be the special purity of the German language and blood, Germans were superior to other races, such as the French, the Spanish, and the Italians, who had been "mongrelized" by intermarriage. "The German is a universal man," he declared," to whom God has given the whole earth as a home."

Like Luther, Arndt linked patriotism with piety. "The highest form of religion," he preached, "is to love the fatherland more passionately than laws and princes, fathers and mothers, wives and children." His emotion-charged writings became standard reading for schoolchildren. One of his

Addressing a crowd of students in 1813, a fiery nationalist speaker calls for volunteers to overthrow Napoléon. Above the painting are Ernst Arndt, Johann Fichte, and Friedrich Jahn *(left to right)*, leaders of the anti-French crusade who preached the racial superiority of the German *Volk* and called for a Führer figure to unite Germany.

patriotic songs, "Was ist das Deutsche Vaterland" (What is the German's fatherland), remained the anthem of the nationalist movement until it was replaced several generations later by "Deutschland, Deutschland über Alles." The song calls upon Germans to create a vast Reich out of all the territories where German is spoken. Until that day arrives, so the lyrics go, Germans will remain unfulfilled.

Another popularizer of the new nationalism was the teacher and youth leader Friedrich Ludwig Jahn, who was born in Prussia and grew up revering the Hohenzollerns. Jahn believed that Prussians were easily distinguished from other Germans by their manly walk, their resolute look, and their forthright speech. "Even little boys at play are already filled with this patriotic spirit," he claimed. "They play more warlike games than do children elsewhere, and if a playmate runs away from a fight, they say: 'That's no true Prussian.'" After meeting Arndt in 1800, Jahn shifted his enthusiasm from the Prussian state to the German people and spent a great part of the rest of his life spreading his nationalistic message. His book *Deutsches Volkstum* (German folkdom) became a kind of proto-Nazi bible. The Germans had become pitiable, he wrote, because they aped French ways. Frederick the Great had created a powerful state, but Prussia collapsed because it was not based on *Volkstum*, a word Jahn coined to convey the mystical, creative force that lies deep within the German soul. He too called for a "Führer cast of iron and fire" to shape Germany's future, claiming "the *Volk* will honor him as savior and forgive all his sins."

In 1811, Jahn organized the first *Turnerschaft*, or gymnastic society. The purpose of its drills and games was to instill an abiding sense of Germanness and prepare his charges, in spirit as well as in body, to fight for the fatherland. In an effort to break down class distinctions, he had the members wear identical gray shirts and address each other with the familiar "du," or "you," rather than in the more formal third-person singular.

While Jahn and his fellow nationalists spread anti-French hatred in the Germanys, Napoléon overreached his power in Russia. After the Grand Army's retreat from Moscow, the new king of Prussia, Frederick William III, took heart. He made an alliance with Russia, Austria, and England, and declared war on France. The resulting War of Liberation united the German states in a common cause for the first time since the Crusades. In October 1813, the allies concentrated their forces at Leipzig and, in the Battle of the Nations, dealt Napoléon a crushing defeat. The remnants of the French army pulled back across the Rhine. Germany was free again.

But the other part of the nationalists' dream—unification—would have to wait. The victorious allies, with the support of the German princes, saw to that at the Congress of Vienna, the international conference called to

remake Europe after the fall of Napoléon. The congress ended in June 1815 just before Napoléon, having escaped from exile on the island of Elba, threatened Europe one final time. After his defeat by British and Prussian armies at Waterloo, the decisions made at the congress went into effect. They disgusted Jahn. He had hoped that the same hatred of the French that had rallied Germans to drive them off their soil would carry over into politics. In Hitleresque fashion, he even made plans for the building of a grand new capital city, called Teutonia, on the Elbe River.

The German princes, anxious to hold on to their power, wanted nothing to do with Jahn's vision. They cooperated with Metternich, Austria's reactionary chancellor, in joining the German states in a confederation under Austria's permanent presidency. Years later, an embittered Jahn cried out: "Germany needs a war of her own. She needs a war against Frankdom to form herself in the fullness of her own folkdom. This time will come; for no people can be born without passing through the pangs of birth."

Jahn's dream would eventually come true—thanks in part to the division of spoils decided upon at the Congress of Vienna. In an irony of history, the delegates deemed Prussia the nation best qualified to keep watch over the stability of Europe. In their wisdom, they granted Prussia, in exchange for ceding Poland in the east, vast new holdings in Saxony, the Rhineland, and Westphalia, moving its center of gravity westward, supplying it with coal and iron for industrial growth, and establishing it as the balance of power against future French aggression.

Jahn renewed his efforts to kindle enthusiasm for unification. He founded the *Burschenschaften,* or national student leagues, under the slogan Honor, liberty, and the fatherland. Their colors were the black, red, and gold of the Lützow Freikorps, a Prussian unit that had been nearly annihilated fighting for the German cause against France. This combination became the colors of the nationalist movement.

To emphasize the simple values of the medieval past, Jahn now dressed in a plain gown of unbleached cloth, which he called the "true German costume." Thus attired, he swaggered through conquered Paris, climbed the Arc de Triomphe, and broke off the trumpet from the mouth of the goddess of victory. Back home, some of his young toughs dressed in bearskins to emphasize their Teutonism. Gangs of them roamed the streets, mocking finely dressed fellow citizens as French toadies.

The national student leagues held their first congress at Wartburg in Thuringia on October 18, 1817. Both the site and the date were carefully chosen: The looming medieval fortress, set high atop a hill, was not only symbolic of the day when knighthood was in flower, it was also where Martin Luther completed his landmark German translation of the New

Flying the black, red, and gold flag of their movement, nationalists battle Prussian troops from behind a barricade in Berlin in March 1848. The uprising led to a constitution that called for a bicameral legislature but gave absolute veto power to the king.

Testament; the year coincided with the 300th anniversary of Luther's revolt, the day with the anniversary of the Battle of the Nations. Thus, by association, Luther and Gebhard von Blücher, the Prussian field marshal who helped defeat Napoléon, were linked to the movement; Luther for his "internal liberation" of Germany, Blücher for freeing Germany "externally."

The highlight of the congress was a torchlight parade that ended with a group of gray-shirted youths throwing books written by antinationalist authors onto a bonfire. The incident, which was supposed to commemorate Luther's burning of the papal bull, shocked the rest of central Europe; a century later, it served as the model for the Nazi book burnings.

Jahn and his followers scattered the seeds of nationalism from a handful of university intellectuals to the broad middle class, but they never won enough support to challenge the old governments reestablished by Metternich. To keep order in the German Confederation, the Austrian imposed censorship and organized a network of spies to report back to him any nationalistic stirrings or calls for political reform. One of his first orders of business was to rid the German states of what he called the "dictatorship of such men as Jahn and Arndt." At Metternich's request, the Prussian government arrested Jahn and closed down his gymnastic societies.

For the next three decades, Metternich maintained a precarious balance of power. But his age of restoration unraveled in 1848 when a wave of

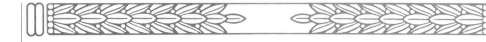

revolutions swept the Continent. That year, the nascent political parties of the German Confederation, inspired by the example of the French, who had forced King Louis Philippe to flee and established a republic, held the first constitutional convention in German history at St. Paul's Church in Frankfurt. Among the elected delegates were two elderly men—Arndt, then seventy-nine, and Jahn, who was seventy. The younger nationalists hailed them as living symbols of their fifty-year-old movement.

The convention was racked by disagreements and, after much debate, produced a mild document that provided for a federal union of the states under the control of a hereditary kaiser, or emperor, with an elected bicameral legislature. Realizing that Austria would never agree, they offered the plan to Frederick William IV of Prussia, who had succeeded Frederick William III in 1840. He contemptuously rejected the idea as a "diadem molded out of the dirt and dregs of revolution, disloyalty, and treason." The king's refusal dealt a deathblow to liberal hopes of developing a German nation-state on democratic lines.

The brief fling with democracy left the liberals bitterly disillusioned. Looking back at the failure, one delegate declared: "The German nation is sick of principles and doctrines. What it wants is power, power, power! And whoever gives it power, to him will it give honor, more honor than he can

Otto von Bismarck, shown at age forty-seven in 1862, when he became prime minister of Prussia, was a master of *Realpolitik*, or practical politics. He broke alliances, abandoned programs, and betrayed supporters in the quest for power.

ever imagine." Another gloomily prophesied: "Freedom and unity cannot come together. Unity must come first and can only be achieved by a tyrant."

But something more compelling than politics was beginning to tug on the Germanys—the Industrial Revolution. As early as 1834, Prussia had begun to reform its customs regulations and later established a *Zollverein*, or customs union, to slice through the maze of tariffs that was strangling commerce among the states. The Prussians cajoled the other principalities to join, giving their nation new leverage over Austria. The rapid growth of capitalism, urbanization, and the middle class helped fuel the momentum, and by the end of the 1850s, Prussia, which nominally had been a constitutional state since December 5, 1848, was gingerly experimenting with parliamentary government.

Nationalist hopes soared when Frederick William IV died and was succeeded by his younger brother William, a soldier by training. To emphasize Prussia's importance, William insisted upon being crowned at the medieval city of Königsberg, founded by the Teutonic Knights, where Brandenburg had been made into the kingdom of Prussia. Like his Hohenzollern ancestors, William's first act was to launch a major expansion of the army and tighten royal control over it. When the legislature challenged his authority to do so, a constitutional crisis developed. William asked his tough-minded ambassador to France for help. That is how, on September 22, 1862, Otto von Bismarck arrived in Berlin, where he was immediately installed as prime minister. For the next twenty-eight years, this son of a Junker landowner and army officer was the effective ruler of Germany.

Bismarck was a conservative even by the standards of the time—so much so that he had sided with Austria in the early skirmishes over control of the German states. He remained a spokesman for absolutism throughout his life, and he never doubted the soundness of his own judgment. "I want to make music the way I like it," he once said, "or else nothing at all." By any measure, Bismarck was an overpowering presence. Carl Schurz, the American journalist and statesman who left his native Prussia after the 1848 failure, described him as "tall, erect, broad shouldered, and on those Atlas shoulders the massive head that everybody knows from pictures—the whole figure making the impression of something colossal."

Despite his imperious personality, Bismarck remained loyal to his king—an attitude rooted in his Lutheran faith. "I am first and foremost a royalist," he said. "I may call him names, and, as a Junker, I can even conceive of rebelling against him. I take the king in my own way, I influence him, trust him, guide him, but he is the central point of all my thinking and all my action, the Archimedes point from which I will move the world."

Bismarck's political ideas were uncomplicated—whatever strengthened

Prussia strengthened Germany, and whatever weakened Prussia weakened Germany. Power, he believed, was the decisive factor in all political issues. He resolved William's crisis over the military budget by simply decreeing that whenever the legislature and the king disagreed about increasing revenue, the government was entitled to levy new taxes and spend the money until agreement was reached. The deputies uttered scarcely a peep of protest. Ferdinand Lassalle, a founder of Germany's first workers' party, used the incident to compare the mentalities of Prussians and Englishmen. In England, he said, if a government agent tried to collect taxes unapproved by Parliament, the citizens would refuse to pay. And if the agent persisted, they would have him arrested. The court would reject the agent's plea of acting on orders and throw him in jail for committing an illegal act. In Prussia the situation was reversed. The citizens would be arrested for "resistance to lawful authority," and the agent praised for doing his duty.

With funds for the army thus assured, Bismarck turned his attention to the longstanding rivalry with Austria. As early as 1856 he had written: "Germany is too small for both of us. Both of us plow the same contested field." He approached the problem obliquely, by engineering a war with Denmark in 1864 for the duchies of Schleswig and Holstein. Afraid to let Prussia expand on its own, Austria joined in the conquest, and for a time both powers shared the provinces. It was a compromise bound to cause dispute, which was exactly what Bismarck wanted. He won the Italians over to Prussia's side by offering to restore Venetia to them, a region the Austrians had seized in 1797. He gained the support of the German states by dangling the prospect of a national parliament. Then he ordered the Prussian troops in Schleswig to expel the Austrians from Holstein.

The war Bismarck manipulated into being was decided within weeks. The Prussians crushed the Austrians at the battle of Königgrätz on July 3, 1866. Bismarck was magnanimous in victory, overruling the generals who wanted to march into Vienna. "The dispute with Austria is decided," he declared. "Now we have to win back the old friendship." By the terms of the peace, Prussia annexed Austria's wartime allies of Hanover, Nassau, Hesse-Kassel, and Frankfurt am Main, eliminating the corridor between the eastern and western provinces of Prussia. These states joined Schleswig-Holstein in a new union called the North German Confederation. The balance of power in central Europe had shifted to Prussia.

The lure of nationalism had superseded the quest for constitutional liberties. Bismarck's popularity soared. "Blood seems to be a peculiar juice," bemoaned the prime minister's Socialist critic, Wilhelm Liebknecht, "for the Angel of Darkness becomes the Angel of Light before whom the people lie praying in the dust. The branding of the breach of the consti-

tution is washed from his forehead, and instead the glorious halo of fame shines from his head crowned by wreaths."

"Germany looks not to Prussia's liberalism but to its power," Bismarck said. "Not by speeches and majority votes are the great questions of the day decided, but by blood and iron." It was a memorable quotation schoolboys would learn by heart. But to fulfill the prophecy, he needed one more war—the long-sought crusade against France.

The provocation for war came when the Spanish throne fell vacant and a German prince from the South German Roman Catholic branch of the Hohenzollern family was put forward to fill it. France, alarmed at Prussia's growing might, protested, and the candidacy was withdrawn. But Napoléon III, the emperor of France, was not satisfied. He instructed his ambassador to extract further guarantees from William I. The Prussian king, who had played no role in the matter, saw no reason to discuss it. Afterward, he sent a routine telegram to Bismarck describing his brief encounter with the French diplomat. Bismarck seized the opportunity. He edited the telegram in such a way that the French would feel insulted and published the text in the newspapers. "It will be known in Paris before midnight," he said, "and not only because of its contents but also because of its mode of publication, it will have the effect of a red cloth upon the Gallic bull." Bismarck's cold-blooded ploy worked: Infuriated, the French declared war.

What the French did not know was that the Prussian army had been preparing three years for just such an event. While Napoléon III bumbled around, summoning reserves from as far as Africa, the German states fell into line behind Prussia and, led by Field Marshal Helmuth von Moltke, launched a surprise attack. Within weeks, the Germans had won a stunning victory at Sedan and captured 120,000 men, including the emperor himself. Napoléon III's debacle led to a republican revolution in Paris, ending the last French monarchy.

The Franco-Prussian War brought to a boil a simmering feud between Bismarck and the Prussian general staff. At issue was control of the army. At first, the prime minister was content to let the generals run the war. But after Sedan, Bismarck wanted to force the French to sue for peace as quickly as possible. He was concerned that Russia might intervene to force a settlement before he had achieved his political goals. Moltke, however, rejected Bismarck's advice as meddling in the army's rightful sphere.

By mid-September, German armies had surrounded Paris. When Bismarck advocated shelling the city into submission, Moltke refused. He considered the French capital no longer a military objective, preferring to save his men for a battle with the remaining enemy forces in the south of France. Nevertheless, Bismarck had his way, and the bombardment was

carried out with ruthless precision. But the line of authority between the general staff and the civil government remained blurry, and the generals never relinquished their prerogative in military matters.

By the spring of 1871, the French capitulated, agreeing to pay Prussia an indemnity of five billion francs and to cede the province of Alsace and parts of Lorraine. Germany had replaced France as Europe's leading power. At the same Versailles Hall of Mirrors where Germany would sign its own humiliating surrender half a century later, King William I was proclaimed emperor, and a Reich formally established with the consent of the other German states. William, in turn, appointed Bismarck chancellor. Many Germans linked Bismarck's creation of the new political entity with the mythical grandeur of the Holy Roman Empire and called the new empire the Second Reich. The poet Franz Emanuel Geibel imagined the imperial throne circled by Barbarossa's ravens, and Richard Wagner called the position of emperor the noblest of all earthly crowns.

A hundred voices joined the chorus of exaltation. The novelist Gustav Freytag saw in the manufactured Franco-Prussian War "the poetry of the historical process." Others claimed a divine hand was at work. "Tears run down my cheeks," wrote the liberal historian Hermann Baumgarten. "By what action have we deserved the grace of God? What for twenty years was the substance of all our wishes and efforts is now fulfilled."

Foreign criticism of German heavy-handedness produced bristling rejoinders. "In view of our obligation to secure the peace of the world, who dares object that the people of Alsace and Lorraine do not wish to belong to us?" Treitschke thundered. "These provinces are ours by the right of the sword, and we shall dispose of them by a higher right—the right of the German nation, which cannot allow its lost children to remain forever alien

German shelling in January 1871 destroyed the heart of Paris, including buildings along the Champs-Élysées *(left)*. Later, victorious German troops paraded in the Place de la Concorde *(below)*. The army occupied northern France until 1873, when the French paid off an indemnity of five billion francs.

to the German Reich." And a weekly magazine commented: "It is easier to accept the smooth superficiality of French civilization in spite of its inner corruption than to appreciate properly the depth of the German spirit. This war has shown that in essentials Germany can never hope to be understood by peoples other than those of German blood."

Bismarck played no role in the chauvinistic outpourings. He pronounced Germany *saturiert*, or satiated, and turned to the practical task of maintaining it. His immediate challenge was to weld together a constitution that

Wearing a white cuirassier uniform, Bismarck looks on as the white-bearded King William I of Prussia is proclaimed German emperor in the Hall of Mirrors at Versailles on January 18, 1871.

fit his special relationship with William I. Bismarck wanted to give the appearance of representative government while reserving independent power for the kaiser—and for himself, through the chancellorship. He accomplished this deftly by making the new Reich a *Bundesstaat*, a kind of federal state. Each state retained its separate identity and control over its own civil affairs. The kaiser ran foreign affairs and was the supreme commander of the imperial armed forces, who swore an oath of allegiance to the kaiser, not to the constitution. Moreover, in his role as king of Prussia, either he or Bismarck, his Prussian prime minister, presided over the Bundesrat, a kind of federal council filled with the princes of the German states. This upper chamber served to mask Prussia's supremacy. As inhabitants of the Reich's largest state, Junkers controlled enough of the council's vote to have veto power over all legislation.

Members of the lower house, the Reichstag, were elected by universal manhood suffrage. But this democratic concession was dampened by the fact that the delegates received no pay and had little authority. The kaiser could convene or adjourn their chamber as he pleased, and the government ministers and chancellor were answerable to him alone. Thus, the half-dozen or so political parties that competed for seats functioned largely as pressure groups to influence legislation or administrative policy on behalf of their own interests. That arrangement suited Bismarck, because it thwarted the very thing he feared most—genuine democracy. The army, meanwhile, remained unencumbered by any constitutional restraints and firmly in Prussian hands. Trying to explain the Reich to a baffled British visitor, the Socialist leader Wilhelm Liebknecht noted wryly: "If you want to understand Germany, you must grasp the fact that Germany is an inverted pyramid. Its apex, firmly embedded in the ground, is the spike on the top of the Prussian soldier's helmet. Everything rests on that."

Bismarck set about making Germany the strongest economic power in Europe, granting generous concessions to industry and creating a stable currency. But he soon found himself threatened by two mass political parties. These were the *Zentrum*, or Catholic Center party, which cut across economic lines and was concentrated mainly in Bavaria, the Rhineland, Silesia, and the Polish provinces of Prussia; and the Marxist-inspired Social Democrats. In Bismarck's eyes, both groups had loyalties stretching beyond German borders, making them dangerous "states within the state."

Bismarck blunted the Social Democrats' appeal by enacting benevolent social legislation ("to take the wind out of their sails," as he put it). Against the Catholics he launched a repressive campaign called the *Kulturkampf,* or the struggle for civilization. "It is not a matter of an attack by a Protestant dynasty upon the Catholic Church," he explained. "What we have here is

the age-old struggle for power between kingship and the priestly class."

He expelled the Jesuits and attacked other teaching orders, insisting that priests be trained and licensed by the state. In Prussia alone, half of the bishops were imprisoned, and more than a thousand parishes were left vacant. Protestant nationalists, alarmed by a recent Vatican encyclical announcing the dogma of papal infallibility, supported repressive anti-Catholic legislation. Yet the Center party flourished, and Bismarck, ever the realist, abandoned his attack—but not before he had inflicted grave damage on an already weak concept of constitutional liberties.

In the diplomatic arena, Bismarck's record was better. With great skill, he created an elaborate system of alliances to maintain a balance of power. The reason for his success, he said, was that "the vision I have is not of the acquisition of some territory but of a total political situation in which all powers except France need us and are deterred from forming coalitions against us because of their relationship to one another." He understood Germany's vulnerable geographic position in the center of Europe. Therefore, as he put it, as long as the world was ruled by an unstable equilibrium of five powers (Germany, Austria, Russia, Great Britain, and France), all politics reduced themselves to this formula: Try to be one of three.

Throughout his years in office, Bismarck had the support of a compliant kaiser. But in 1888, at the age of ninety-one, William I died. He was succeeded by his fifty-seven-year-old son, Frederick III, the husband of Queen Victoria's eldest daughter. Frederick was a great admirer of British parliamentary institutions and dreamed of remaking Germany along democratic lines. During the Franco-Prussian War, he had noted in his diary: "I maintain even today that Germany could have 'conquered morally,' without blood and iron. It will be our noble but immensely difficult task in the future to free the dear German fatherland from the unfounded suspicions with which the world looks upon it today. We must show that our newly acquired power is not a danger but a boon to humanity." Unfortunately, he did not live to implement his ideas. He died of throat cancer ninety-nine days after assuming the throne.

Frederick's twenty-nine-year-old son became the new emperor, William II. Young William despised his father's liberal thinking. He hated constitutionalism and political parties. (He would later call the members of the Reichstag "a troop of monkeys and a collection of blockheads and sleepwalkers.") He also resented Bismarck's power and refused to subordinate himself to the aging chancellor. As he saw it, God had appointed him to lead his people. "The new kaiser," sighed Bismarck, "is like a balloon. If you don't keep hold of the string, you never know where he'll be off to." Another observer noted dryly, "His Majesty's autocratic tendencies are not accom-

After Prussia and the South German states that were allied with it defeated France in 1871, the Prussian statesman Otto von Bismarck merged four kingdoms, six grand duchies, five duchies, and seven principalities into a German empire under the Prussian king, William I, who became emperor of the Second Reich. Although the constituent states retained varying degrees of autonomy, Germany was, for the first time, a unified nation.

panied by any serious scrutiny of the facts; he just talks himself into an opinion. Anyone in favor of it is then quoted as an authority, anyone who differs from it is 'being fooled.'"

Almost immediately, the headstrong young emperor and the strong-willed old chancellor locked horns over social legislation. William II favored it. He had come to the throne imbued with the nationalistic values of the Christian-Social movement led by Adolf Stöcker, a demagogic evangelical pastor, who equated worker exploitation with Jewish capitalism. Bismarck opposed further concessions to labor. But the final falling-out came over their relationship as king and prime minister of Prussia. To limit William II's exposure to the ideas of others, Bismarck dug up a dusty decree, signed

A Career Satirized in Cartoons

Otto von Bismarck's imperious style, bald pate, and ample girth made him irresistible to cartoonists, as this international sampling shows:

1 Bismarck, as the goddess Victory, drives the chariot atop the Brandenburg Gate.

2 As Pope Leo XIII extends his foot to be kissed, Bismarck offers him his boot.

3 Bismarck as the unyielding disciplinarian of the Reichstag.

4 The chancellor strains to keep a lid on Germany's labor parties.

5 As a winsome farmer's daughter, Bismarck throws crumbs to his pet nations.

6 Dropping the pilot from the German ship of state as a self-satisfied William II looks on.

7 In retirement, the leviathan continues to spout his opinions.

BISMARCK AS "THE FARMER'S DAUGHTER"

by Frederick William IV in 1852, obliging Prussian ministers to consult with the prime minister before approaching the king. Infuriated by this unsubtle effort to control him, William II ordered Bismarck to repeal the decree or resign. The embittered old man chose resignation and on March 17, 1890, retired to his Friedrichsruh estate in Schleswig-Holstein.

Although the kaiser announced that the course would remain the same, he quickly shifted the focus of foreign policy. Not content with being dominant on the Continent, he set out to transform Germany into a global power with a colonial empire and a powerful navy. The new emphasis suited the muscle-flexing mood of the day. Germany was enjoying an era of unprecedented growth, and most citizens saw in the kaiser's

Bismarck welcomes the new kaiser, twenty-nine-year-old William II, to his Friedrichsruh estate in 1888. "His inexperience can lead to no good," the aging chancellor said. "He is much too conceited."

Weltpolitik, or world policy, an outlet for their boundless energies.

Contributing to the public's uncritical acceptance was the resurgence of a virulent form of racist nationalism, epitomized by the *Alldeutsche Verband*, or Pan-German League. Founded in 1890, the league embraced the notion that pureblooded Teutons were the creators and bearers of civilization and thus responsible for all worldly progress, while Jews were a corrupting, negative force—a dogma popularized by Houston Stewart Chamberlain, the Anglo-German author and son-in-law of Richard Wagner. The league's professed goal was to gather all the lands they considered German into a huge union. These included the Netherlands, Belgium, Luxembourg, Switzerland, Hungary, Poland, Rumania, Serbia, and Austria. From this enlarged Reich, the Pan-Germans intended to rule the world. Although many observers considered the league the lunatic fringe of German nationalism, its membership included many of the Reich's most

Well-wishers bid Bismarck farewell at Berlin's Lehrter railway station after his resignation in 1890. "He left behind a nation without political will," a critic wrote, "a nation accustomed to submit to anything decided for it."

respected military, industrial, government, and university leaders.

The racist, antidemocratic writings of Paul Anton de Lagarde, Julius Langbehn, and Heinrich von Treitschke also shaped the German mentality. Lagarde, who insisted that "democracy and culture are mutually exclusive," was disappointed in Bismarck's Reich because it had not been sufficiently racially pure and paid too much lip service to parliamentary government. He longed for a new Reich, led by a Führer who "by some mysterious intuition, educates his nation in its needs." Langbehn shared Lagarde's views. In his best-selling book *Rembrandt as Educator*, in which through curious leaps of logic he proclaims the humane Dutch painter the source of German racist nationalism, he calls for a "new Barbarossa, a Caesar-artist whose fire of spirit and strength of arm will fulfill our ancient, victorious longings." The widely read Treitschke popularized the glorification of war as a means to achieve German greatness. He predicted that a new German empire would replace the old British Empire and subjugate the Slavs of central Europe. "Those who proposed the foolish notion of a universal peace," he declared, "show their ignorance of the international life of the Aryan race." William II himself frequently attended Treitschke's political lectures.

The kaiser's penchant for bombast sharpened a growing worldwide fear of Germany. He peppered his speeches with references to Germany's "place in the sun," its "mailed fist," and "glistening coat of mail." When he dispatched troops to help deal with the Boxer Rebellion in China, he instructed them to behave like the merciless Huns of Attila. And when the British prime minister, Herbert Asquith, tried to discuss the balance of power on the Continent, the kaiser replied, "There is no balance of power in Europe but me—me and my twenty-five corps."

At the kaiser's order, Admiral Alfred von Tirpitz began a massive ship-building program designed to match the British navy ship for ship. It apparently never occurred to either emperor or admiral that such an audacious plan would drive Britain into the arms of its traditional foe, the French. The friction with the British over naval armaments was only one of many conflicts. Relations with the Russians also soured, and they too turned toward France. One by one, Germany forfeited friendships, until finally it was left with the crumbling Austro-Hungarian Empire as its only reliable ally. In 1909, Chancellor Theobald von Bethmann-Hollweg summed up the kaiser's foreign policy: "Challenge everybody, get in everyone's way, and, in the course of it all, weaken nobody."

Long before this total deterioration of Bismarckian balance, the leaders of the army, worried that Germany faced encirclement by hostile neigh-

On parade, officers and troopers of the Garde du Corps, the emperor's bodyguard cuirassiers, wore a silver imperial eagle on their lobster-tailed helmets. For ordinary duties a spike was substituted. The helmets were made of tombac, an alloy that gave the appearance of gold.

Symbols of Imperial Tradition

Mounted Rifles wore a blued steel cuirassier helmet with a dragoon-pattern eagle. A member of the 8th Regiment wore this one.

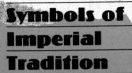

This sealskin busby of the Guard Hussars originated with seventeenth-century Hungarian mercenaries.

Battle honors for service in Spain with the Duke of Wellington adorn the eagle on the shako of the 10th Hanoverian Rifle Regiment.

In German households, a profusion of beer steins, statuettes, and certificates emblazoned with the motto *In Erinnerung an meine Dienstzeit* ("In commemoration of my time in service") were reminders that imperial Germany was a nation of draftees. Young men viewed military service as a proud obligation. Hence, uniforms served not only to clothe but also to symbolize martial valor and tradition.

For most soldiers, some form of the spiked helmet, introduced by Prussia in the 1840s, was standard headgear. Each kingdom placed its royal arms on the helmets, and old-line regiments added battle honors and devices recalling heroics of long ago. Bright facings of regimental colors and lace decorated the uniforms; then, in 1910—foreshadowing the depersonalized war to come—the army issued a less visible combat uniform in dull field gray (*see following pages*).

A cord attached to a 13th Uhlan Regiment lancer's cap kept him from losing it while mounted. The helmet plate bears battle honors of the Napoleonic Wars, including Waterloo.

This Foot Artillery Regiment helmet is embellished with a cannonball in lieu of a spike.

The helmet and undress cap of the 92d Braunschweig Infantry Regiment bear the skull and crossbones of the black-uniformed Braunschweig Corps of 1809. The striped shoulder-board piping indicates that the tunic was worn by a young man with a student or other deferral who served only one year.

Issued to the 105th Saxon Infantry in 1910, this field uniform, which was intended for wear on maneuver and in time of war, retained the cut and details of the dress uniform. The ornate helmet came with a field gray cover.

The light gray-green jacket of the *Jäger-zu-Pferd,* or Mounted Rifles, was patterned after the tunic worn by cuirassiers. The broad stripe of braid came in a different color combination for each regiment and concealed hooks and eyes.

The 108th Saxon Rifle Regiment wore this dark green tunic and Austrian-style kepi. The sunburst cap plate bore the arms of Saxony and a rifleman's bugle. The regiment wore horsehair plumes on parade.

bors, had begun moving to take control of national policy. While Tirpitz was getting his first naval program approved, Count Alfred von Schlieffen, chief of the army general staff, was creating a risky plan for a two-front war against France and Russia. It called for a powerful right wing to smash through neutral Belgium and Holland, outflank the French defenses, and wheel south to envelop Paris, while a skeletal force defended the eastern frontier against the Russians. After swiftly finishing off the French, the Germans would attack the Russians. When Schlieffen presented his ideas to the government and announced that he intended to ignore diplomatic treaties, the civilian ministers capitulated immediately. They assured him that if the chief of the general staff considered such a measure imperative, it was "the duty of diplomacy to concur."

By 1914, the army's thirst for a "preventative war" had gathered widespread support, and control of foreign policy had quietly passed to the general staff. After the assassination of the Austrian Archduke Francis Ferdinand at Sarajevo touched the match to the final crisis, Germany found itself in a race. When the Russians announced their decision to mobilize on July 29 and the French followed suit on August 1, the pressure on the kaiser intensified. If he failed to mobilize, the Schlieffen plan would be imperiled. The very size of the army compelled a decision: From some 250,000 men in 1870 it had grown to two million strong, and the timetable for moving such an overwhelming force left no margin for delay.

Germans welcomed William's mobilization order with giddy excitement. When Carl Zuckmayer, a young writer, claimed that Germany was correct in refusing to bow before the "pressure of a world opposition that would deny it the free unfolding of its energies," he voiced the sentiments of the vast majority of his fellow citizens. Zuckmayer described being infected with war fever: "Then, in the enormous Cologne station droning with song, marching steps, the cries of travelers, it went through me like the radiation of a current of cosmic electricity. It transposed the body as well as the soul into a trancelike, enormously enhanced love of life and existence, a joy of participation, a feeling, even, of grace." Even the opposition joined in the frenzy. The Socialist Konrad Haenisch claimed that at first he felt trapped between the "burning desire to throw oneself into the powerful current of the national tide" and the horror of betraying his own principles. "Suddenly—I shall never forget the day and the hour—the terrible tension was resolved," he recalled. "One could join with a full heart, a clean conscience, and without a sense of treason in the sweeping, stormy song: 'Deutschland, Deutschland über Alles.'"

But under the timid leadership of Helmuth von Moltke, nephew of the strategist of Sedan, a modified Schlieffen plan failed to produce a quick

Britain's Queen Victoria *(front row, center)* is surrounded by royal relatives in a rare 1894 photograph. William II, Victoria's grandson, is at far left in the front row; his cousin, Czar Nicholas II of Russia, is second from left in the second row; and William's uncle, who became King Edward VII of England, is at far left in the third row.

victory. The advance into France was stopped at the Marne in September. Now Germany faced a two-front war of attrition. Months-long slaughters ensued at sites such as Verdun, yet over the next three years the western front never shifted by more than ten miles. Meanwhile, Germany won great victories in Russia and the Balkans. Through all this time, the kaiser's High Seas Fleet sat idle, bottled up in the Baltic by the British navy.

In 1916, when Field Marshal Paul von Hindenburg took over as chief of the general staff and his former chief of staff General Erich Ludendorff became first quartermaster general, Germany became a virtual military autocracy. The collapse of Russia in the 1917 revolution brought a surge of optimism as well as vast territories in the east. The civilian population, fed an unvaried diet of Germany's victories and ignorant of its defeats, was

confident that the army would prevail. In fact, it was bleeding to death.

In the fall of 1918, after the last great German offensive had been broken at the second battle of the Marne, Prince Max of Baden formed a new government to formulate a response to Allied surrender demands. One condition was the resignation of William II. "A descendant of Frederick the Great does not abdicate," fumed the kaiser. But his world was clattering down about his head: Prince Max demanded and got Ludendorff's resignation; on October 27, Austria quit the war; when Admiral Reinhard Scheer ordered the High Seas Fleet to sea, mutiny broke out among the sailors, and similar uprisings were beginning to occur within the army.

The final drama was played out at the royal estate in the town of Spa on the raw, damp afternoon of November 9, 1918. Informed by General Wilhelm Groener, Ludendorff's successor, that the army would "march home in good order under its generals but not under Your Majesty," the kaiser retreated: He would resign the imperial throne, but remain the king of Prussia. It was too late. Prince Max had already announced the abdication and turned the government over to the Socialist Friedrich Ebert. That night, William II slipped away into Holland. "Treason, gentlemen! Barefaced, outrageous treason!" he had shouted. The end had come with such suddenness that people felt betrayed. When peace terms were announced that saddled them with the onus of responsibility for the war as well, the soil was prepared for a generation warped by vengeful bitterness. ✠

Jubilant Berliners celebrating the outbreak of war in August 1914 hold aloft pictures of William II and his ally, Emperor Francis Joseph I of Austria-Hungary. "For us," wrote one enthusiast, "the war is the most sacred thing on earth."

The kaiser (*second from left*) stands with Germany's wartime leaders, including the supreme commander, Field Marshal Paul von Hindenburg (*far left*), and his brilliant deputy, General Erich Ludendorff (*second from right*).

A Decisive Gamble on the Western Front

By the fourth grueling year of the Great War, imperial Germany's resources were stretched to the breaking point. Germany's trade had been crippled by the British naval blockade, its armies bled white by attrition. When the United States entered the conflict on the side of the Allies, defeat seemed only a matter of time. But German hopes revived when Russia collapsed in revolution and civil war. After the new Bolshevik government signed the Treaty of Brest-Litovsk on March 3, 1918, hundreds of thousands of German soldiers were freed for service in the West.

In the spring of 1918, the German high command embarked on a last desperate gamble for victory—a massive offensive aimed at breaking the costly three-year stalemate on the western front and bringing the war-weary Allies to the negotiating table before American forces could arrive in strength. This so-called Peace Offensive, code-named Michael, was the brain-child of Quartermaster General Erich Ludendorff, widely regarded as the German army's master strategist. Ludendorff determined that the British forces should be the principal target of the offensive, believing them to be "less apt than the French to support a defensive battle on a large scale."

At 4:40 a.m. on March 21, 1918, ten thousand German guns and mortars opened fire on the British trenches and supply lines. Despite stringent German security, the British had suspected that a large-scale offensive was imminent. They were unprepared, however, for the volume and accuracy of the shelling. Five hours later, 800,000 German soldiers swept forward on a front forty-three miles long in what Winston Churchill called the greatest onslaught in the history of the world.

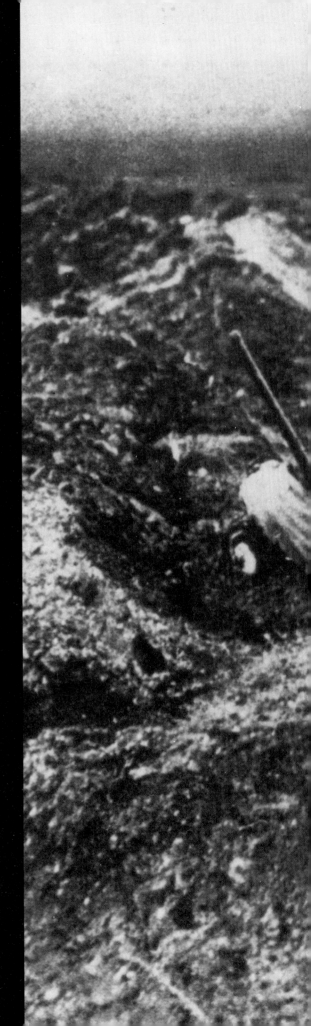

German soldiers marshal in their trenches before the start of Ludendorff's great offensive. "The tension was almost unbearable," one veteran confessed. "Nagging doubts overcame us."

The Graveyard of Idealism

Although they had marched to war filled with idealism and patriotic fervor, the soldiers manning front-line trenches on the western front had lapsed into a fatalistic stupor by 1918. Struggling to survive in a ravaged moonscape reeking with the stench of poison gas and decaying corpses, theirs was a daily ordeal of unrelieved and unmitigated horror. It was as though the war had taken on a life of its own, consuming lives and hopes in what the British officer-poet Robert Graves called the sausage machine.

With neither side able to attain a clear strategic advantage over the other in the face of deadly modern weaponry, the average German soldier cherished little hope for the success of Ludendorff's offensive. One eighteen-year-old German conscript confessed that he "felt like bursting with anger" at the continued carnage and waste of trench warfare. "Oh, you poor nation!" he lamented. "This is how you settle your politics."

A slain German soldier, face
stripped to the bone by rats,
sprawls beside an abandoned
dugout. Once buried, the dead
were frequently unearthed
again by enemy shellfire.

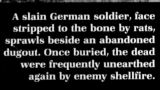

German troops wander through
the blasted landscape near
the town of Ypres, Belgium.
"Here the villages are merely
names," an officer wrote.
"Even the ruins are ruined."

47

Advance of the Storm Troops

Ludendorff's offensive made deadly use of shellfire and poison gas. But the initial success of Michael was due primarily to a dramatic new tactic: following up the bombardment with fast-moving, specially equipped units called *Sturmabteilungen*, or storm troops.

Wearing gas masks and armed with flamethrowers, light machine guns, and grenades, the storm troops moved out well in advance of the main German assault, infiltrating and spreading confusion through the Allied lines. Larger battle groups followed the storm troops, with instructions to exploit every breakthrough. "The reserves must be put in where the attack is progressing," Ludendorff ordered, "not where it is held up."

Hastily donning gas masks, German soldiers scramble to their combat positions. On March 21, the attackers advanced behind a lethal cloud of poison gas.

Firing from a flatcar (*right*), a ▷ 380-mm gun supports the German offensive. The largest of these cannons shelled Paris from a seventy-five-mile range.

A squad of storm troops rushes to the attack. These small, elite units played a crucial role in the offensive and suffered commensurate casualties.

A Taste of Victory

Ludendorff's gamble paid off: The spring offensive met with unprecedented success. In the first four days, the Germans gained more territory than the Allies had in three years of fighting. Nearly a hundred square miles of territory and 21,000 prisoners fell into German hands.

By June, German forces had reached the Marne River, on the outskirts of Paris. One officer exulted that "victory called from every corner." But at this critical point the offensive ground to a standstill.

German losses had been heavy, supply lines were stretched perilously thin, and discipline began to give way as hungry soldiers abandoned the fight to pillage captured

Continuing the westward drive, a German column marches across the old battlefield of the Somme, a region in northern France that had been devastated when the German army withdrew the previous year.

Repeating their charge through
shell-torn woods for a camera,
troops of the U.S. 23d Infantry
Regiment advance under the
covering fire of a 37-mm gun.

Traveling by automobile,
truck, and horse-drawn cart,
a newly arrived American
observation-balloon company
(right) heads toward the front.

A Transfusion of Yankee Blood

By the end of July 1918, the arrival of nearly a million and a half American troops had bolstered the depleted Allied ranks. A jaded French officer compared the deployment of the American Expeditionary Force to the "magical operation of the transfusion of blood." Under the leadership of a newly appointed commander in chief—Marshal Ferdinand Foch of France—the Allies now took the offensive.

The Yanks played a crucial role in checking the German advance on the Marne, then forged ahead in costly victories at Saint-Mihiel and the Argonne Forest. Scornful of static trench warfare, the Americans wanted, as one New Yorker put it, to "get out in the open and slug it out." The Americans gave the Allies the boost they needed to turn the tide of the war. "They have come here to do and die and are as keen as mustard," a British soldier wrote. "They are in truth Crusaders."

A battalion of New Zealanders advances behind a British tank during the Allied counteroffensive in the summer of 1918.

A youthful German conscript ▷ emerges from his dugout (right) and surrenders to British troops during the July 1918 battle for Rheims forest.

German artillery fire scores a direct hit on a British Mark IV tank (below) during the pivotal battle of Amiens.

Black Day for an Overmatched Army

In the predawn hours of August 8, 1918, British, Canadian, and Australian divisions lashed out furiously at the wavering German forces along a fourteen-mile front at Amiens. The Allied assault was supported by low-flying aircraft and spearheaded by an armored phalanx of 604 British tanks.

Although tanks had been a part of the Allied arsenal since 1916, they had rarely been used to advantage as one element of a coordinated strategic operation. At Amiens, however, the tanks exceeded all expectations, blasting through the German lines and crushing diehard defenders beneath their massive treads. "August 8 was the Black Day of the German army," Ludendorff wrote. "The army ceased to be a perfect fighting instrument."

Defeat's Bitter Harvest

Thousands of German prisoners fill an Allied compound (*left*). "Their soldiers are no more than a pitiful crowd," a Scottish sergeant wrote. "They are marked with the sign of the defeated."

Following the armistice, demobilized German soldiers throng a homebound train. They returned to a nation in chaos, its political and social institutions shattered.

The sudden collapse of the German army shocked friend and foe alike. Entire divisions disintegrated as the Allies swept eastward toward the German frontier. Disheartened by the failure of their offensive, their ranks depleted by battlefield losses and ravaged by a deadly influenza epidemic, the German soldiers lost the will to continue the struggle. "The troops deteriorated both spiritually and physically," a Bavarian officer lamented. "For the most part they were burned-out cinders."

Social and political unrest swept the German home front. Agitation by revolutionaries spawned a series of crippling strikes, soldiers and sailors mutinied, and finally the German people began to turn on their leaders.

After General Ludendorff's resignation on October 26, his replacement, General Wilhelm Groener, declared, "Loyalty to the flag is now a fictional concept." The November 11 armistice put an end to four years of slaughter on the western front, but left a legacy of bitterness in a Germany whose next battles would erupt from within.

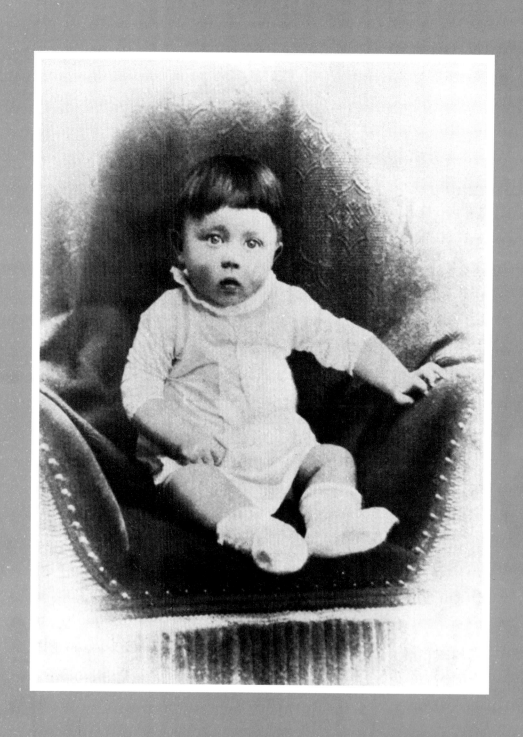

TWO

The Education of an Outsider

Today it seems to me providential that Fate should have chosen Braunau am Inn as my birthplace," wrote Adolf Hitler of the Austrian village on the German border where he was born in 1889. "In this little town on the Inn River, Bavarian by blood, Austrian by nationality, lived my parents in the late eighties of the past century; my father a dutiful civil servant, my mother giving all her being to the household, and devoted above all to us children in eternal loving care."

Thus begins *Mein Kampf* (My struggle), Hitler's political autobiography and blueprint for a new Germany. From the deliberately portentous, sentimental notes struck by those opening lines, the story the future Führer tells of his own life bears the stamp of a fairy tale. It begins with the birth of a sensitive, artistic boy, who even in playground games demonstrates a precocious grasp of the arts of war. By the age of eleven, he is a committed nationalist who has learned to "understand the meaning of history." Orphaned and impoverished at eighteen, the protagonist of this fable is forced to earn his bread and seek his fortune in a harsh world. From his subsequent years of hunger and manual toil and his intensive study of the great political thinkers of history comes the inspiration for a unique and sweeping political program to match his vision of a glorious Germanic future.

The account is as contrived as it is romantic. Throughout his life, Hitler consistently lied about his background, manipulating the facts to present himself as the incarnation of what he judged the German people yearned for in a leader: a mythic figure risen from humble beginnings to triumph over adversity and seize his destiny as the head of a mighty nation. He took pains to ensure that no other version should ever leak out. The press, he told an indiscreet nephew in 1939, "are not to know who I am. They are not to know where I come from or what my family background is."

Some members of Hitler's inner circle inferred from the Führer's insistence on obscuring his antecedents that there was some dark secret in his past. One sensational though flimsy theory held that he was hiding a Jewish grandfather. The facts were more prosaic. Hitler's childhood was not much different from those of many other middle-class Austrian boys

Less than a year old, the infant Adolf Hitler sits calmly in a photographer's velvet-covered studio chair, his crisp white garments attesting to the meticulous care of a doting mother.

of his generation, and as he grew into an unhappy and aimless adolescence, the only destiny that seemed to await him was persistent failure and obliterating obscurity. He spent his early adult years as a would-be art student, surviving on money from his family and a fraudulently obtained orphan's pension; when those sources ran dry, he accepted charity rather than stoop to manual labor. His political education and the ideology that resulted from it were profoundly self-centered, motivated purely by the need to find answers for tormenting and overwhelming personal problems. His search took him not to the great minds of German history but to the purveyors of the most disreputable racist fanaticism that was thrown up in the turbulent final years of the Austro-Hungarian Empire. It was on the fringes of a decaying society that this disturbed, solitary, and powerless figure assembled what he would call the "granite foundation" of his political program—a doctrine based on hatred, revenge, and the desire to see subjugated people prostrate at his feet.

Given his psychology and the facts of his upbringing, it is little wonder that Hitler contrived a heroic version of his background. In the end, he may have half believed it himself. In any event, to him it was preferable—and certainly more useful—than the truth.

Austria's remote Waldviertel, or forest area, lies northwest of Vienna, near the border of present-day Czechoslovakia. The land there was stingy, offering only a meager living. Their countrymen considered the inhabitants of this harsh region inbred, suspicious, and hardheaded, with an iron stubbornness developed from centuries of struggle in their isolated valleys.

Adolf Hitler's grandmother, Maria Anna Schickelgruber, was born in 1795 to a family whose hardscrabble lives followed the pattern of generations of Waldviertel peasants. From the little that is known of Maria Anna, it appears that she left her village as a young woman to work as a domestic servant and returned in 1837, at the age of forty-two, pregnant and unmarried. Her son Alois was born that June.

Maria Anna refused to name her baby's father, and the child's birth was recorded as illegitimate in the parish register of the nearby village of Döllersheim. A century later, this domestic mystery would emerge to haunt Adolf Hitler with rumors that his grandmother had been made pregnant by the son of a Jewish family by whom she was employed. At the time, however, most of Maria Anna's neighbors assumed that the baby had been fathered by Johann Georg Hiedler, an itinerant mill worker she married five years after Alois's birth. Later, when the boy was sent off to live with Hiedler's brother, Johann Nepomuk Hiedler, a farmer, local gossips whispered that he was the one who had fathered Maria Anna's child.

Hitler adored his mother, Klara, a modest, gentle woman, and as an adult he kept her picture with him at all times. His father, Alois, a domineering, punctilious bureaucrat who styled his mustache like that of his emperor, Francis Joseph, inspired a turbulent combination of fear, awe, and angry defiance in the boy.

Whatever their blood ties may have been, the farmer raised Alois as a son, arranging for his schooling and an apprenticeship to the village shoemaker. But the child had higher ambitions for himself, and when he was thirteen, he ran off to Vienna. At that time, Europe was adjusting to an industrial economy. A new middle class was forming, and with it opportunities were arising that had not existed for peasant boys a generation earlier. Chances for advancement were particularly abundant in the Austro-Hungarian Empire, which stretched from Switzerland in the west to Russia in the east. A labyrinthine bureaucracy that produced thousands of jobs grew up to administer this vast and unwieldy realm.

Alois entered the system as a member of the customs service. He worked hard, rose steadily, and in 1875 was made a full inspector of customs at Braunau am Inn. This was an exceptional achievement for a boy from the Waldviertel, and in 1876 old Johann Nepomuk Hiedler, apparently as an expression of pride in the young man he had raised, called on the Döllersheim parish priest and asked that Alois be declared the legitimate offspring of his brother Johann Georg Hiedler. The farmer and three companions each swore that Johann Georg—who, along with Alois's mother, had long since died—had told them this was the case. In a highly irregular procedure, the priest altered the baptismal record to make Alois a legit-

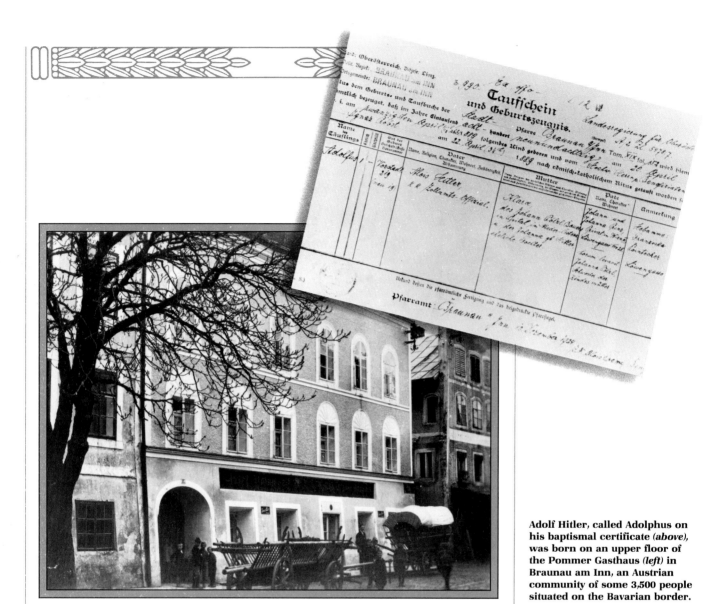

Adolf Hitler, called Adolphus on his baptismal certificate *(above)*, was born on an upper floor of the Pommer Gasthaus *(left)* in Braunau am Inn, an Austrian community of some 3,500 people situated on the Bavarian border.

imate member of the Hiedler clan. The four illiterate witnesses were not aware that the rustic cleric, going by the pronunciation sometimes used for Hiedler, had spelled the family name "Hitler." Nor did it bother Alois. His newly minted name was an important symbol of middle-class respectability, confirming his hard-won status as a member of the bourgeoisie—despite his having a remarkably messy domestic life.

Alois was a freewheeling womanizer who had already sired an illegitimate child before his marriage in 1873 to an invalid fourteen years his senior. Not long after the wedding, he impregnated the nineteen-year-old kitchenmaid of the Braunau gasthaus where he and his wife lodged. The young woman had given birth to his son and was pregnant with his daughter by the time Alois's wife died in 1883. He promptly married his mistress, even though by then he had begun an affair with young Klara Polzl, daughter of his foster sister Johanna Hiedler and granddaughter of his benefactor, Johann Nepomuk Hiedler.

Klara became the third Frau Hitler in 1885 after Alois's second wife died. She was a quiet girl, with brown hair and startlingly pale blue eyes. Her life was sad. She loved her two stepchildren, Alois junior and Angela, but her own three babies all died in infancy. Her husband—Uncle Alois, as she called him—gave her scant comfort. "No kid gloves as far as they were

Draped with a Nazi banner after Hitler's rise to power, the house in Leonding where he lived from ages ten to sixteen *(top)* stands adjacent to the cemetery where his parents are buried. Other childhood homes include the large farmhouse in Hafeld *(left)* where his family lived for two years after his father's retirement in 1895, and the apartment building in Linz *(right)* where his mother died in 1907.

concerned," recalled a family friend, describing Alois's treatment of Klara and the children. "His wife had nothing to smile about."

Klara's fourth child was born on an overcast Easter eve, April 20, 1889. Christened Adolf, he was a sickly, fretful baby. His mother watched over him obsessively and shielded him from his quick-tempered father. Adolf grew into a thin, dark-haired boy with an angular face dominated by his mother's penetrating blue eyes. In 1895, the year his father retired, the six-year-old Adolf started school in the village of Hafeld, one of several way stations for the family before it finally settled in Leonding, a suburb of Linz. A quick pupil, he breezed through his work, earning high marks. Outside the schoolroom, he was an energetic playmate who reveled in devising imaginative projects—noisy war games featuring heroic German soldiers, or cowboy-and-Indian adventures inspired by the stories of Karl May, a

convicted forger and con man whose lurid tales of the American West had made him one of Germany's most popular writers.

Adolf's home life was far less happy. Alois ran his household like a boot camp, never sparing the rod. The children were not allowed to speak in his presence without permission, and he insisted on being addressed formally, as "Herr Vater," instead of by the familiar and affectionate "du." Alois junior, who bore the brunt of these oppressive attentions, ran away from home in 1896, leaving his younger siblings at the mercy of their tyrannical sire. These now included Adolf's brother Edmund, age two, and infant sister, Paula. Adolf, now seven, had inherited his father's hair-trigger temper as well as his obstinacy; the clashes between the two were explosive. Years later, Paula recalled that her brother's rebelliousness "challenged my father to extreme harshness," and as a result, Adolf "got his sound thrashing every day." From hints that Hitler himself would later drop, his father's brutal treatment left him simmering with the repressed anger and inchoate desire for revenge that are the classic legacy of a beaten child.

In 1900, the year his brother Edmund died of the measles, Adolf turned eleven. He entered a *Realschule,* one of Austria's technical and scientific secondary schools and the generally accepted entryway into professions such as engineering and to certain technical posts in the civil service. For the first time in his academic career, he faltered badly. His grades were so poor that he was required to repeat most of his first-year courses, and even then he barely squeaked by. Hitler later explained his miserable performance in high school as a deliberate attempt to sabotage his father's ambitions for him. Alois, he claimed, wanted him to enter the civil service, but young Hitler had decided on a career as a painter. "My father was struck speechless. 'Artist, no, never as long as I live!' He forbade me to nourish the slightest hope of ever being allowed to study art. I declared that if that were the case, I would stop studying altogether."

The account has a ring of truth. Since the senior Hitler revered the Austrian civil service, it would have been entirely in character for his son to spurn it out of hand. Yet it is also true that Hitler, who had always coasted effortlessly through his schoolwork, lacked the self-discipline needed to buckle down and master the secondary school's demanding curriculum. One of his teachers later recalled the "gaunt, pale-faced youth" as "notoriously cantankerous, willful, arrogant, and irascible. He had obvious difficulty in fitting in at school. Moreover, he was lazy. His enthusiasm for hard work evaporated all too quickly. He reacted with ill-concealed hostility to advice or reproof; at the same time, he demanded of his fellow pupils their unqualified subservience, fancying himself in the role of leader."

Yet Hitler's new classmates were noticeably cool toward him. His school

Ten-year-old Adolf *(top row, center)* gazes haughtily from his elementary-school class picture, exhibiting a cocky self-assurance that would soon dissolve under the pressures of high school.

was located in Linz, three miles and a world away from the Leonding village green where he had lorded it over crude farm boys. While he eventually was able to lure some of the younger pupils into his games of cowboys and Indians, a widening gulf separated him from boys of his own age. No longer the brightest, the most talented, the unquestioned leader, he was an increasingly miserable and lonely youth who cloaked his resentment beneath an aloof and touchy exterior. He was particularly scornful of his teachers—"erudite apes," he later labeled them—whose sole mission was to persecute and repress talented, creative boys such as himself.

The only teacher to escape Hitler's youthful disdain was his history professor, Dr. Leopold Poetsch, an ardent German nationalist and active local politician who served on the Linz town council. Poetsch was a disciple of Georg Ritter von Schönerer, radical leader of the Austrian Pan-German party. Unlike the association of the same name in Germany, Schönerer's movement was less concerned with Germany's need to expand its colonial empire than with unifying all Germans under one state. His aim was the establishment of a German-dominated Austria that would merge with Prussian-dominated Germany.

Schönerer and his followers idolized Germany's "Iron Chancellor," Otto von Bismarck, and despised Austria's ruling Habsburg dynasty for granting equality to the empire's non-German ethnic groups. The Pan-Germans were virulent anti-Semites. Fearful of the uncertainties and changes of modern life, they also embraced the *völkisch* doctrine, yearning for a political program that would return them to a pure Germanic culture based on the eternal verities of home and soil.

Such sentiments were widespread during Hitler's school days, but they had particular resonance among German-speaking Austrians, who felt themselves an increasingly threatened minority in the polyglot Habsburg empire. In an atmosphere of fear and uncertainty, Professor Poetsch's illustrated lectures on the ancient Teutons found a particularly receptive audience. "Even today, I think back with gentle emotion on this gray-headed man," Hitler wrote in *Mein Kampf,* "who, as if by enchantment, carried us into past times and, out of the millennial veils of mist, molded dry historical memories into living reality."

Hitler was not sufficiently inspired by his favorite teacher to undertake a serious study of German history, however. Despite his professed enthusiasm, his grades in history were not much better than his other marks. But Poetsch's lectures contributed an important element to the fantasy life of the alienated youth, who was increasingly inclined to retreat into his imagination to escape his domineering father and his academic failures. At the same time, young Hitler absorbed the attitudes and catch phrases

In a scene from Hitler's favorite opera, *Lohengrin,* by Richard Wagner, the pure-souled knight Lohengrin bids farewell to his lady love, Elsa, and departs to search for the Holy Grail. Hitler was so taken with this tale of ancient Teutonic warriors that he memorized the entire libretto.

of the extreme nationalists and loudly proclaimed his devotion to "Germandom." The fact that anti-Habsburg sentiments were an integral part of Austrian Pan-Germanism added to its appeal for him, providing Hitler with another way to get at his father, the devoted imperial servant.

These sentiments dovetailed neatly with another crucial influence that entered his life. When Adolf was twelve, he attended his first opera, a performance of Richard Wagner's *Lohengrin*. It ignited a lifelong passion for the composer and for the blood-and-fire-filled pageantry of his musical dramas. Wagner's works proved even more potent than Adolf's imagination in transporting the boy into the histrionic dream world of primitive German legend—a land of mystic vapors, epic clashes, dragon slaying, pagan sexuality, treachery, and redemption. In the dark stalls of the Linz Opera

House, he could see himself as Siegfried or Parsifal, a heroic Germanic warrior destined to lead a great people.

Then, on January 3, 1903, the real life of the thirteen-year-old boy took a dramatic turn. That morning, Alois visited his favorite gasthaus and was taking his first sip of wine when he toppled over, felled by a massive pleural hemorrhage. He was dead before the doctor arrived.

Hitler would later say that his father's death subjected the family to deep economic privation. In fact, Alois left his wife and children well provided for. Besides a pension and a yearly allowance for Adolf and Paula, there were cash legacies and the house in Leonding, which Klara sold in 1905, adding the proceeds to her comfortable capital reserves. She moved her family into a rented apartment in Linz.

That fall, sixteen-year-old Adolf, still foundering academically, left school without receiving his graduation certificate, the diploma needed to advance to a higher institution. He resisted all efforts to steer him into a job and proceeded to "prepare" himself for his chosen career in art by reading, sketching, and daydreaming. With his mother and his little sister to wait on him, he affected the life of a young gentleman of leisure. He slept until midday and loafed for most of the afternoon. In the evenings, he emerged carefully dressed and, carrying an ivory-tipped ebony cane, strolled alone down Linz's main promenade, the Landstrasse, presenting a thin, pallid picture of troubled adolescence and youthful pretension.

The only person who was impressed by this foppish would-be artist and dandy was a similarly lonely boy named August Kubizek, who met Hitler when the two were competing for standing room at the opera. An aspiring musician who worked in his father's upholstery shop during the day, "Gustl" was a naive boy who, from the moment he laid eyes on Hitler, saw a figure of transcendent glamour. "He belonged to that particular species of person of which I had imagined myself a member in my more expansive moments: an artist, one who despised the mere bread-and-butter job and devoted himself to writing poetry, to drawing, to painting, and to going to the theater," wrote Kubizek many years later. His

parents were somewhat less enthusiastic about their son's peculiar new companion. "What eyes your friend has!" said Frau Kubizek after meeting young Hitler for the first time. Gustl admitted that Adolf was a difficult friend—humorless, moody, and fiercely possessive. And yet, he claimed, being at Adolf's beck and call was a small price to pay for being included in all of his enthralling and grandiose schemes.

Apart from attending the opera, walking was the friends' main occupation. As they took their long afternoon and evening tramps—often not returning before two or three in the morning—Hitler would hold the other boy spellbound with his monologues, many of which dealt with plans for rebuilding Linz. "He could never walk though the streets without being provoked by what he saw," recalled Gustl, relating how Hitler would stand in front of a structure and launch into a windy architectural critique, then pull out his drawing pad and scratch away furiously to produce an improved design. If the more practical Kubizek ventured to ask his friend how he intended to carry out his plans, Hitler impatiently brushed the query aside. "His belief that one day he would carry out all his tremendous projects was unshakable."

One evening, as the boys were taking their customary stroll down the Landstrasse, Adolf suddenly gripped Kubizek's arm and pointed to a slender, fashionably dressed blond girl walking decorously at her mother's side. "You must know, I'm in love with her," he declared dramatically. Too timid to approach the girl directly, Hitler commissioned Kubizek to inquire about her among his student and musician acquaintances. Gustl soon reported that her name was Stefanie and that she had a good soprano voice—something that Hitler, who had mentally already cast her as all his favorite Wagnerian heroines, claimed to have known instinctively.

"Stefanie filled his thoughts so completely that everything he said or did or planned for the future was centered around her," according to Kubizek. Hitler wrote poems to the girl, dreamed about their wedding, and spent endless hours designing a house for her. Although he never spoke a word to her, he insisted that she shared his feelings. For two such exceptional human beings, he declared, there was no need for ordinary communication; extraordinary people understood one another intuitively.

Hitler's faith in Stefanie's love survived even when he jealously observed her chatting with young officers. He chose to interpret her gaiety as a subterfuge to hide her own tempestuous feelings for him. And yet, the thought of her in the company of other men so disturbed him that he finally decided to kidnap her in order to "rescue" her. The alarmed Gustl succeeded in persuading Adolf that the plan was impractical, only to have his friend hatch an even more appalling scheme—a dramatic double suicide

The young woman known as Stefanie, the unwitting object of Hitler's romantic obsession, was astonished when informed years later of his infatuation. It was only then that she realized it must have been Hitler who wrote the strange letter she had once received; it came from an unidentified admirer who told her he planned to marry her after finishing his art studies.

in which he and Stefanie would drown side by side in the Danube.

The innocent object of these disturbing fantasies remained totally unaware of them, because Hitler never followed through on his youthful schemes—concerning Stefanie or anything else. He never translated his rough architectural sketches into finished drawings. For all his professed interest in politics, he never joined in the heated partisan political activity of the day. His feverish town planning, his music criticism, his fulminations over the state of the world—none went any farther than the ears of his loyal audience of one.

Perhaps the most active attempt he made in those days to translate his dreams into reality was to buy a lottery ticket. Confident he would win, Hitler located a spacious apartment for him and Kubizek to share and mentally decorated it in "refined, personal taste." Their new home would be the center of a circle of art lovers, he said. A distinguished elderly lady would be employed to run the establishment and greet their select and lofty-minded guests. The two gifted young gentlemen would make regular trips to Vienna to attend lectures and concerts. In the summer, they would tour Germany and go to the annual Wagner festival at Bayreuth.

When the day of the lottery drawing arrived and someone else won, Hitler was beside himself. "First he fumed over the state lottery, this officially organized exploitation of human credulity, this open fraud at the expense of docile citizens. Then his fury turned against the state itself, this monster built by Habsburg marriages. Could one expect other than that two poor devils should be cheated out of their last few kronen?"

Fifty years later, Kubizek speculated that his boyhood friend's uncontrollable anger on this and other occasions reflected a deep, inconsolable unhappiness. "He saw everywhere only obstacles and hostility," wrote the still-sympathetic Gustl. "And yet nobody had ever heard of him. Sometimes I was even sorry for him. With his undoubted gifts, what a happy life he could have led; and how difficult he made things for himself! He was always up against something and at odds with the world."

Hitler continued on his aimless path, mooning over Stefanie and restlessly spinning his fantasies. But pressure was building for a change. Klara, already deeply concerned about her difficult son's future, was being urged

"I have been working very hard, often till two, even three, in the morning," Hitler wrote on a postcard from Vienna to his friend and roommate August Kubizek (*above*), who was spending the summer of 1908 in Linz. A few years earlier, visiting Vienna for the first time and eager to share his impressions, Hitler had sent Kubizek a card showing the interior of the Opera House (*opposite, top*), which he described as "overloaded" with gold and velvet, and another of the weapons collection at the Art History Museum (*opposite, below*).

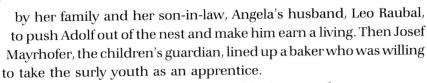

by her family and her son-in-law, Angela's husband, Leo Raubal, to push Adolf out of the nest and make him earn a living. Then Josef Mayrhofer, the children's guardian, lined up a baker who was willing to take the surly youth as an apprentice.

Such a prospect appalled Hitler, and he became desperate to escape. He had visited Vienna for two weeks in 1905 and had dreamed ever since of studying art there. He begged his mother to let him go to the capital and enter its Academy of Fine Arts. In the summer of 1907, no longer able to resist his impassioned pleading, Klara allowed Adolf to withdraw from the Mortgage Bank of Upper Austria all of the money he had inherited from his father. It was enough to cover his tuition at the academy and support him for a year. He left Linz that September.

Hitler arrived in the cosmopolitan Habsburg capital confident and self-assured. Then he took the entrance examination for the academy and was rejected. Reeling from what he called this "bolt from the blue," he asked the director of the academy for an explanation. "That gentleman assured me that the drawings I had submitted showed my unfitness for painting. The place for me was the School of Architecture." But Hitler could not enroll in the architecture school without a graduation certificate, and it evidently did not occur to him that he might return to secondary school to obtain one. Stymied, he lingered indecisively in Vienna, letting his family believe he was enrolled at the academy. Apparently, he returned home only when his mother died on December 21, 1907. It was a shattering blow. Klara's uncritical love had been the only reliable prop to his fragile emotional existence. The family doctor later wrote that in all his career, he had "never seen anyone so prostrate with grief as Adolf Hitler."

Linz was now unbearable. In addition to his anguish over the loss of his mother, there were the sharp inquiring looks and embarrassing questions about his studies from his relatives and his detested brother-in-law. In February 1908, as soon as his mother's estate was settled and twelve-year-old Paula installed with the Raubals, Hitler returned to Vienna. Later that month, Kubizek joined him and took up studies at the Conservatory of Music. The two lived together in a rented room on Stumpergasse, a noisy street of bargain-basement shops not far from the busy Westbahnhof, the depot for express trains from Munich and Paris.

For the rest of his days, Hitler would recall his sojourn in Vienna as the unhappiest time of his life. "For me the name of this Phaeacian city represents five years of hardship and misery," he wrote in *Mein Kampf.* "Five years in which I was forced to earn a living, a truly meager living that never sufficed to appease even my daily hunger."

But for the first two of those years, Hitler never had to lift a finger to earn his way. By keeping quiet about his academic status, he continued to receive his orphan's pension, which would last until he was twenty-four if he gave the impression he was a legitimate student. The pension, plus his patrimony and a legacy from his mother, gave him an income of some 80 to 100 kronen a month. It was more than enough to allow him to live frugally and to attend the opera, which he did almost nightly, as if drugging himself on the music and spectacle.

During the day, he stalked restlessly though the streets, occasionally dropping into public libraries to read whatever the whim of the moment suggested. Driven by his preoccupation with the alleged defects of the world, he devised fantastic schemes to remedy them. He invented a non-alcoholic drink, drew up plans to reform the school system, and composed wordy tracts attacking landlords and officials. He sketched theaters, castles, and exhibition halls, and even tried to write an opera.

Kubizek, familiar with his friend's moods and fancies, sensed something alarming in all this frenzied activity. "I had the impression in those early days in Vienna that Adolf had become unbalanced. He would fly into a temper at the slightest thing. Choking with his catalog of hates, he would pour out his fury over everything, against mankind in general, which did not understand him, which did not appreciate him, and which persecuted him." For a time, Hitler pretended even to Gustl that he was in school; when he admitted to his roommate that he had been rejected by the academy, he launched into a truly terrifying tirade. "His face was livid, the mouth quite small, the lips almost white. But the eyes glittered. There was something sinister about them. As if all the hate of which he was capable lay in those glowing eyes."

In September 1908, while Kubizek was on a trip home to Linz, Hitler mustered up his courage and presented himself again as a candidate for admission to the academy. This time his sample drawings were deemed too poor even to qualify him to take the entrance examination. Unable to admit his latest failure to his one friend, he moved out of their apartment and disappeared into the city, leaving no forwarding address.

Hitler moved into new lodgings at 22 Felberstrasse, an area of cheap boardinghouses in southwest Vienna. His inheritance was dwindling, but

the money would last almost another year. During that time, he made no effort to get a job but continued his life as a student without a school.

Alone, adrift, and consumed by a need to find any explanation for his failures other than his own shortcomings, Hitler began to search in earnest for answers. Above all, he needed an enemy to blame, and it did not take him long to find one. As he related in *Mein Kampf,* he was walking along the street one day when he "suddenly encountered an apparition in a black caftan and with black earlocks. Is this a Jew? was my first thought. I observed the man furtively and cautiously, but the longer I stared at this foreign face, scrutinizing feature for feature, the more my first question assumed a new form: Is this a German? As always in such cases, I now began to try to relieve my doubts by books. For a few hellers I bought the first anti-Semitic pamphlets of my life."

Hitler had an abundance of literature to choose from as he embarked on this fateful new direction in his studies. Vienna was arguably the most anti-Semitic city in western Europe. Beginning in the middle of the nineteenth century, a stream of Jewish immigrants had migrated to the capital from the more repressive eastern parts of the empire. Between 1857 and 1910, the Jewish proportion of the population rose from two percent to more than eight percent, higher than in any city in central Europe.

The ethnic Germans, already feeling threatened by the non-Germanic population, reacted to the influx of Jews with fear and resentment. They were particularly repelled by the immigrants' Eastern customs and style of dress. To many Viennese, the conspicuously alien appearance of these new city residents seemed to support the then-fashionable thesis that Jews were a biologically different species from Germans. This spurious theory had popped up like a weed in the scientific flowering of the nineteenth century, providing a racial basis for anti-Semitism that augmented centuries-old economic and religious prejudices. According to the *völkisch* agitators, the Jews were a desert-derived race—intellectually dry and spiritually barren. Germans, on the other hand, who had supposedly risen from the verdant, mist-enshrouded forests, were an instinctive, romantic, and profound people. In these stereotypes, Jews were regarded as intrinsically hostile to the German *Volk.* Moreover, another school of dubious nineteenth-century science, Social Darwinism, held that all races were in competition with one another for livelihood. German-speaking Austrians noted with suspicion the preponderance of Jews in occupations such as banking, teaching, and journalism, and concluded that they were deliberately sabotaging German culture.

From all these elements arose the concept of a grand conspiracy, with Jews engaged in a multipronged attack on German values, economy, and

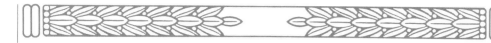

racial integrity. By the turn of the century, this theory had penetrated deep into the intellectual fabric of German-speaking Austria and won adherents in all segments of society. Organized anti-Semitic groups abounded, and anti-Semitism was the rallying cry for rival political organizations from Schönerer's Pan-Germans to the dominant Christian Socialist party, led by Vienna's popular mayor Karl Lueger.

Hitler's education in anti-Semitism and Social Darwinism came principally from Vienna's gutter press, which by the early 1900s had concentrated the racist currents of the day into a torrent of hate literature. In a tobacco shop near his new residence, Hitler picked up the scurrilous periodical *Ostara*, the official publication of a secret society called the New Temple. Its founder was a former Cistercian monk named Adolf Lanz, who went by the nobler-sounding name Georg Lanz von Liebenfels. He lived in a ruined castle in Upper Austria, where he led a fanatic band of enthusiasts in mystical chants to the stars and the Teutonic spirits (including Ostara, the Teutonic goddess of spring).

Human existence, according to Lanz, revolved around the elemental mortal conflict between two groups: heroic blond, blue-eyed Aryans and their racial inferiors, the "Dark Ones." A large category encompassing blacks, Slavs, and Jews, the Dark Ones were uniformly depicted in *Ostara* as hairy, apelike subhumans, possessed of both cruel cunning and an overpowering sexual potency. *Ostara* was filled with pornographic tales of blond women falling into the clutches of the swarthy ape-men, polluting the Aryan race with their unbridled rapacity. Added to this heated sexual emphasis was a large dose of the occult, including numerology and old Germanic spells. The pages of *Ostara* were spangled with runic symbols and signs from ancient legend—including the hooked cross, or swastika.

Although Lanz was too far detached from day-to-day concerns to provide Hitler with an entirely satisfying philosophy, he pointed the way toward a more focused pamphleteer, Guido von List, leader of an association called the List Society. Whereas Lanz saw threats to German culture virtually everywhere, List zeroed in on the "hydra-headed international Jewish conspiracy" as the mortal enemy of Germandom and concocted a detailed prescription for its defeat.

List wrote that it would take a great world war to annihilate what he characterized as the "mongrelized brood that destroys customs, religion, and society." The way to prepare for the conflict, he argued, was to build a strong, racially pure state—an Aryan Reich. List outlined the structure of this Reich: It would be divided into *Gaue*, or districts, each headed by a gauleiter bound by secret oath to a supreme leader, or Führer, who would be the "visible embodiment of the divine Aryan law." The new Reich would

The dome of the eighteenth-

century Karlskirche—modeled on St. Peter's in Rome—looms over a bustling Vienna in this tinted photograph taken about 1900.

City of Failed Dreams

Of the city where he had hoped to fulfill his youthful dreams, Adolf Hitler once wrote, "Vienna represents the memory of the saddest period of my life." Attracted in 1907 by the bright cultural lights of the imperial capital, the boy from Linz found only disillusionment beneath the glamorous facade. After two rejections by the Academy of Fine Arts dashed his artistic ambitions, he made a meager living by selling postcards that he had painted. Desperate to blame his failures on someone else, the embittered young man lashed out at foreigners and Jews. As his despair deepened and poverty loomed, his hatred broadened to include almost all segments of Viennese society. "He wallowed deeper and deeper in self-criticism," a friend wrote. "Yet it needed only the slightest touch—as when one flicks on the electric light—for his self-accusation to become an accusation against the times, against the world."

Hitler collected scapegoats from the entire spectrum of Viennese society *(represented clockwise from the near right)*. Fashionably dressed couples only reminded him of his failed courtship of a young girl in Linz. Of Vienna's Jews, the future Führer wrote, "Was there any form of filth or profligacy, particularly in cultural life, without at least one Jew involved in it?" Avant-garde artists were destructive hedonists rather than purveyors of German culture. He considered imperial soldiers mere props of a moribund empire whose end was hastened when Emperor Francis Joseph granted equal rights to non-Germans. Slavic servant girls epitomized the threat that foreigners posed to a pure Aryan Germany, and middle-class matrons in hired carriages only sharpened Hitler's awareness of his own deprivation. His roommate wrote, "Wherever he looked, he saw injustice, hate, and enmity."

have special marriage laws to prevent the mixing of races, and each household would be required to maintain "blood charts," a kind of family studbook detailing racial background that would be available for examination by government authorities on demand. Other statutes would suppress inferior people and force them into slavery. "Only members of the Aryo-Germanic humanity of masters enjoy the rights of citizenship," List decreed. "Members of inferior races are excluded from all positions of influence and authority."

By and large, Lanz and List were considered extreme even by the viciously racist standards of prewar Vienna. Athough *Ostara* enjoyed a fairly broad readership in Austria and Germany, it drew most of its following from the fringes of society. It was especially popular in the down-and-out circles in which Hitler now moved—the lost, anonymous men who inhabited cheap rooming houses on the outskirts of the city. The pseudoscientific style of New Temple and List Society literature, along with its pornographic elements, its emphasis on secret rituals and symbols, and its advocacy of extreme solutions for complex social ills—all made compelling reading for an audience predisposed to suspect that there were obscure explanations for the world's problems.

For Hitler, grappling with his own problems, the discovery of a hidden Jewish conspiracy working its influence on affairs everywhere was galvanizing. At one stroke, he was supplied with a simple, reassuring explanation for every setback and failure. He devoured the works of Lanz and List and even tracked down Lanz in person to obtain back issues of *Ostara*.

At about this time, Hitler also discovered the popular German author Theodor Fritsch, extolled by his publishers as the "creator of handy anti-Semitism." Fritsch's *Handbuch der Judenfrage* (Handbook of the Jewish question) had gone through twenty-six printings by the time Hitler arrived in Vienna and joined its legion of readers. Like Lanz and List, Fritsch believed that the Jews—in alliance with Catholics, Freemasons, and Jehovah's Witnesses—were plotting worldwide domination, and he documented his thesis with an eye-popping array of purported evidence.

Fritsch compiled long lists of Jewish writers, publishers, musicians, and artists to support his contention that they were corrupting German culture en masse. He gathered statistics on the preponderance of Jewish physicians and warned that they posed a menace to the health of German children. *Handbuch der Judenfrage* also claimed to prove the extent of Jewish criminality, methodically listing the names of hundreds of Jews who allegedly were responsible for all of the major crimes committed in Germany for the past century, from murder and rape to treason and forgery. Fritsch combed the writings of famous historical figures for anti-

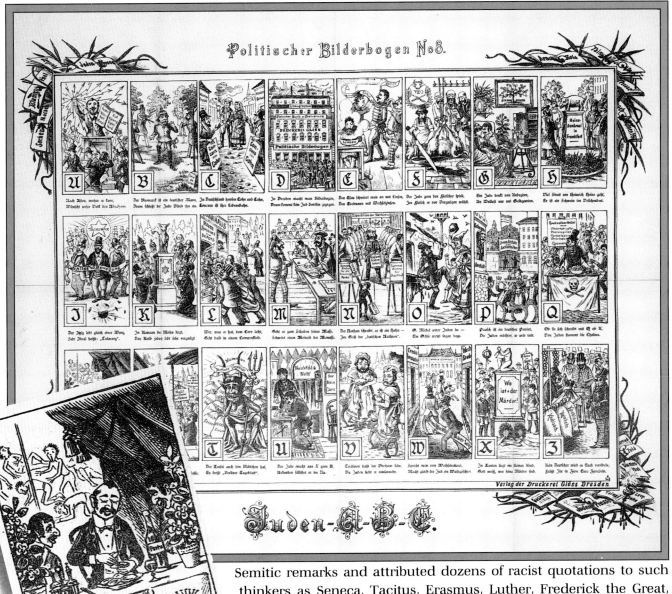

A cartoon called "The Jewish ABCs," a typical example of the anti-Semitic propaganda in wide circulation during Hitler's youth, insultingly catalogs purported Jewish racial characteristics. The letter *R*, for example, depicts a member of the Rothschild banking dynasty eating oysters and reads: "In Russia where starvation reigns, Rothschild eats up a storm."

Semitic remarks and attributed dozens of racist quotations to such thinkers as Seneca, Tacitus, Erasmus, Luther, Frederick the Great, Voltaire, Goethe, and Edward Gibbon, among others.

For Hitler, Fritsch's handbook was a treasure chest to which he returned time after time to rummage for nuggets of supposedly factual information. Other than his pamphlets and periodicals, it was his principal text in Vienna. He was so taken with Fritsch that in 1931 he wrote a dedication to a new edition of the handbook that praised its author for providing what he called "factual proof" of the Jewish menace. The book later would become officially sanctioned reading in German schools after Hitler came to power.

The works of Georg Lanz von Liebenfels and Guido von List would fare less well in what passed for intellectual life in Nazi Germany. Although page after page of *Mein Kampf* was to read like thinly paraphrased issues of *Ostara*, and the Third Reich, down to its swastika emblem, would echo the forms and rituals of the New Temple and the List Society, Hitler would be so intent on presenting himself as the sole creator of national socialism that he would never concede his considerable debt to his two key mentors.

In fact, there was only one person whom Adolf Hitler ever freely and fully acknowledged as a major influence on his life and thought: Richard Wag-

ner. From the moment he heard the opening strains of *Lohengrin* as a schoolboy, Hitler worshiped the composer. "For me, Wagner is something godly, and his music is my religion," he told a reporter in the 1930s. "I go to his concerts as others go to church." It was more than Wagner's thrilling operatic renditions of German myth that inspired this idolatry. Hitler was equally captivated by the composer's views on race, politics, art, and religion. It is not clear when he first encountered Wagner's essays, but they were available throughout Austria during Hitler's youth and were collected in Vienna's municipal libraries, where he pursued his various scattershot research projects. Eventually, he would boast that he had read everything the master had ever written.

Wagner was as prolific a writer as he was a musician. But while his musical compositions bore the ennobling stamp of genius, his prose seemed to be drawn from the same well of hatred as the jottings of Lanz, List, and Fritsch. A fervent German nationalist, Wagner had been one of the nineteenth century's more visible and vocal exponents of racial anti-Semitism and the doctrine of Social Darwinism. He regarded as his own great contribution to those philosophies his unique ability to assert, on his authority as a creative genius, that Jews were incapable of creating great music, literature, or visual art.

From his home in Bayreuth, Wagner published an anti-Semitic periodical dedicated to the creation of a pure Germanic state. Readers of the *Bayreuther Blätter* learned that all the noble impulses of history were Aryan, that the decline of civilization was due to pollution by Jews and other alien races, and that salvation lay in the emergence of a great leader who would establish a racially pure society and achieve the "resurrection of the German *Volk*." Wagner also advocated the enslavement of so-called inferior peoples, arguing that it was "quite justified in the natural sense" for the superior race to dominate and exploit the inferior ones.

As if such ringing confirmation of his own views from so revered a source were not enough for Hitler, the Master of Bayreuth also provided him with inspiration in a host of other areas. Wagner considered himself an authority on virtually every conceivable subject, from diet and exercise to Shakespeare and Hegel. A vegetarian, he combined unusual solicitude for the welfare of animals with brutal indifference to human suffering. Throughout his life, Hitler studied and parroted Wagner in these areas as he did in politics. "I have the most intimate familiarity with Wagner's mental processes," he said. "At every stage of my life I come back to him."

Hitler's irregular studies were interrupted in mid-1909, soon after he turned twenty, when he ran through the last of the money he had inherit-

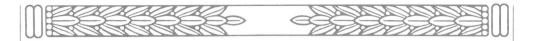

ed from his parents. The monthly orphan's pension was not enough to cover the cost of both his meager meals and the flophouses he slept in, and as summer turned into a cold and rainy autumn, on many nights he slept shivering on park benches. Shortly before Christmas, he wearily made his way to the Meidling district on the outskirts of the city and joined a long line of destitute men and women at the doors of the Obdachlosenheim, a cavernous shelter for the homeless maintained by a Viennese charitable society. It represented the end of the line, the last refuge for those who had exhausted all hope. Tired and hungry, his threadbare clothes streaked by the chemicals used at the shelter to disinfect vermin-infested garments, Hitler sat silently on his wire cot, so abjectly miserable that even some of the other vagrants felt sorry for him and tried to lend him a hand.

Under the prodding of one of them, a drifter named Reinhold Hanisch, Hitler pulled himself together and wrote home for money. An aunt promptly sent him fifty kronen, which the pair used to move out of the shelter and into a more comfortable men's hostel across town. With some of the money they set themselves up in a small business. Hitler painted watercolor postcards of Vienna street scenes copied from photographs, Hanisch sold them, and the two men split the profits. The partnership enjoyed a modest success. By the time it broke up, over a dispute in which Hitler had Hanisch arrested for allegedly cheating him, there was a certain demand for the young painter's work. From 1911 to 1913, Hitler settled down to more or less systematic production as a petty businessman on the fringes of the art world. His expenses were low, and he made just enough money to support himself. He also now had time to resume his self-directed education, and he returned to his polemical pamphlets and periodicals with new enthusiasm. "A thousand things that I had hardly seen before now struck my notice, and others that had previously given me food for thought I now learned to grasp and understand," he declared pompously of his intellectual endeavors during those years.

Hitler claimed that this was the time when he discovered the true extent of Jewish influence in all spheres of life, from the press, where he "detected the accents of a foreign people," to the streets, where he recognized the Jew as the "shameless and calculating director" of prostitution and white slavery. Finally, he said, the scales truly dropped from his eyes when he concluded that Jews were the instigators and backers of Marxism.

During this same period, Hitler began to observe contemporary politics with a fresh eye. None of the established parties had the precise combination of ideological elements to attract his allegiance. Rather, he poked away at the spectrum of political thought to pick out elements he found interesting or useful. The nationalistic, *völkisch* platform of Pan-

Germanism provided him with a basic political framework. Vienna's Mayor Lueger, a supremely pragmatic politician and a charismatic leader who had deftly exploited anti-Semitic sentiments for his political purposes, provided a superb model of the successful demagogue. Even the Marxist Social Democrats had something to teach him, opening his eyes to the importance of mass party organization and the indispensability of propaganda. "In a few years, I thus created for myself the basis of the knowledge on which I still feed," Hitler wrote in *Mein Kampf.* "During that time I formed a picture of the world and an ideology that has become the granite foundation of my deeds. I had only to add a little more knowledge to that which I had acquired at the time; I did not have to revise anything."

The core of Hitler's philosophy was anti-Semitism and a belief in the inequality of races and individuals. Around it he assembled a related stock of fixed ideas and prejudices: a preference for authoritarian government coupled with contempt for the principles of democracy and a hatred of Marxism and internationalism. As he put it, "The Jewish doctrine of Marxism rejects the aristocratic principle of nature and replaces the eternal privilege of power and strength with the mass of numbers."

This collection of attitudes and ideas was yet to come into focus, but all of the elements were in place by early 1913, when Hitler moved to Germany. "My inner aversion to the Habsburg state was increasing daily," he wrote of his decision to leave Vienna. "This motley of Czechs, Poles, Hungarians, Ruthenians, Serbs, and Croats, and always the bacillus that is the solvent of human society, the Jew, here and there and everywhere—the whole spectacle was repugnant to me." He did not mention that he would be leaving behind an obligation that he had avoided thus far. Under Austrian law he should have registered for military service when he turned twenty. He had failed to do so and had also ignored the requirement to report for duty annually over the three following years. Because he had never been tracked down, he evidently concluded that he had escaped his military obligation. He assumed that after his twenty-fourth birthday, in April 1913, the Austrian draft board would have no more say in his future, and he could leave the country without danger of pursuit from the authorities.

On May 24, 1913, he packed his scanty belongings in a single piece of hand luggage and set off for Munich. From the moment he stepped off the train in the Bavarian capital and breathed the fresh air blowing down from the nearby mountains, Hitler felt at home. "The city was as familiar to me as if I had lived for years within its walls." He was seized with a heady infatuation. "A German city! How different from Vienna."

Hitler found lodgings above a tailor's shop. The next day he bought paints and an easel and set to work. He soon discovered the market for

His rapturous face captured in an unguarded moment by a news photographer, Hitler mingles with the crowd in Munich's Odeonsplatz on August 2, 1914, to hear the German proclamation of war. "Overpowered by stormy enthusiasm," he later wrote of the moment, "I fell down on my knees and thanked heaven from an overflowing heart."

commercial art was much smaller in Munich than in Vienna, and the only way he could sell his paintings was to peddle them door-to-door or in beer halls. Even this humiliation failed to dampen his enthusiasm. Hitler was living the artist's life in the city where Wagner had composed *Tristan and Isolde, Die Meistersinger,* and *Das Rheingold,* and nothing could dim its magic glow. Munich would always be his favorite city, the place where he had first known the "happiness of a truly inward contentment."

Hitler remained in this euphoric state right up to the Sunday afternoon in January 1914 when he was arrested by the Munich police, who bore an order from Austrian authorities for him to report immediately to the Linz draft board. He was informed that he would be prosecuted if it was found that he had left the country to evade conscription.

Confronted by the real danger of a prison sentence, Hitler was terrified. By the time he was taken, under guard, to the Austrian consulate the following day, he was on the verge of collapse—so shaky that the consul took pity on him and appended a note of support to his desperate and cringing letter begging the Linz draft authorities for mercy. The consul then arranged for the trembling draft dodger to report to nearby Salzburg rather than to Linz. Two weeks later he appeared before the draft board and was given a physical examination. "Unfit for combat and auxiliary duties, too weak. Unable to bear arms," was the verdict.

He returned to Munich and continued to eke out a living as a painter for the next five months, until June 28, when Archduke Francis Ferdinand, the Habsburg heir, was assassinated, igniting a world war. Hitler volunteered for duty the day Germany declared war on France, petitioning to serve in the forces of Bavaria even though he was an Austrian citizen. To his joy, he was accepted and assigned to the 16th Bavarian Reserve Infantry Regiment.

Hitler's unit, called the List Regiment after its original commander, was filled with students and young professionals, exactly the type of educated, upper-crust young German whose company he had always craved. He was determined to prove himself, and from the beginning he compensated for his frail physique with an ardor for all things military. On the second day of basic training, another recruit watched Hitler holding his new rifle. "He looked at it with delight, as a woman looks at her jewelry."

The List Regiment first saw combat that October in the first battle of Ypres, in which the British repulsed an all-out German effort to break through to the Channel coast in Flanders. The engagement became known as *der Kindermord bei Ypern*—"the slaughter of the innocents at Ypres." In a letter to his landlord in Munich, Hitler reported that in four days, the strength of his regiment had been reduced from 3,500 to 600 men.

The unsuccessful attempt to take Ypres ended the German offensive and marked the beginning of four years of trench warfare. Hitler became a regimental courier, carrying dispatches between the front lines and regimental headquarters. It was a dangerous job, but it suited his solitary personality, and he discharged his duties with courage and exemplary zeal. In December 1914, he was decorated for bravery, winning the Iron Cross, Second Class. In 1918, he received an even greater distinction, the Iron Cross, First Class—a rare honor for an enlisted man. Exactly what Hitler

During his tour of duty at the front, Hitler wore the oval metal disk identifying him as a member of the 1st Company of the 16th Bavarian Reserve Infantry Regiment. Convalescing from a wound in the winter of 1916-17, he carried a military pass (*above*) **indicating that he was assigned to the 2d Bavarian Infantry Regiment, with which he drew light duty in Munich before returning to the front.**

Thin and drawn, his mustache waxed into military points, Corporal Hitler stands stiffly beside two fellow infantrymen and a mascot. "I passionately loved soldiering," he later said, referring to the war as the "greatest and most unforgettable time of my earthly existence."

did to earn the decorations has never been made clear. The regimental history does not mention his deeds, and Hitler never provided details—possibly because he was recommended for the honors by a Jew, the regimental adjutant, Hugo Gutmann. Nevertheless, they were genuine badges of exceptional achievement, the first he had ever received, and he was thrilled. The fact that he had earned the honors in combat, the arena respected above all others by Germans, made it even more wonderful. Later, the badges would prove invaluable to the Austrian Hitler's career, granting him a sort of spiritual German citizenship and lending legitimacy to his participation in German politics.

Hitler loved the army. Indisputably, he now belonged—sharing the prestige of a great and feared institution he had admired since childhood. For the first time in his life, he had purpose and direction as well as a structure that provided an outlet for his restlessness while appealing to his sense of solemnity. He had never felt so completely at home. "For Corporal Hitler, the List Regiment was his homeland," wrote one of his superior officers perceptively. On the whole, he even got along well with his fellow soldiers, although they considered him something of an eccentric. Unlike the others, Hitler sent and received few letters, seemed indifferent to women, and did not share in the ordinary soldiers' griping. When he worried aloud, he expressed suspicions of betrayal and anxieties over invisible foes. "He is just an odd character and lives in his own world," said one of his comrades.

In October 1918, the List Regiment had returned to the Ypres sector when the field kitchen Hitler was standing in was hit by British shells containing chlorine gas. Temporarily blinded, he was sent to a hospital in Pomerania. It was there, on November 11, that he heard the devastating news that Germany had capitulated. "I tottered and groped my way back to the ward," he wrote, "threw myself on my bunk, and dug my burning head into my blanket and pillow." He was sobbing. The blow was as sudden and incomprehensible to him as his rejection by the Academy of Fine Arts, and as staggering as the death of his mother. He would look back on that day as the most critical of his life and refer to it ritualistically as the moment of his great political awakening. "If this hour of trial had not come, hardly anyone would have guessed that a young hero was hidden in this beardless boy," he wrote of himself. "The hammer stroke of fate, which throws one man to the ground, suddenly strikes steel in another." At the time of Germany's surrender, however, he was merely numb, facing the future with no idea of what his place in it would be. "There followed terrible days and even worse nights—I knew that all was lost," Hitler was to write. "Only fools, liars, and criminals could hope for the mercy of the enemy. In these days hatred grew in me, hatred for those responsible for this deed." ✚

Portrait of a Marginal Artist

Sketched by a schoolmate around 1905, when his own artistic ambitions burned brightest, the adolescent Hitler appears as a thin, awkward youth with the wispy beginnings of a mustache.

"Test drawing unsatisfactory. Not admitted." That was the verdict of Vienna's Academy of Fine Arts when eighteen-year-old Adolf Hitler applied to study there in 1907. But the customers who bought Hitler's paintings and drawings in the following years passed a more favorable judgment on his ability. Beginning in 1910, when he set up a postcard-painting business with fellow drifter Reinhold Hanisch, Hitler supported himself as a commercial artist. That he made only a marginal living at it was evidently due more to a lack of ambition than of talent; his exasperating tendency to dawdle infuriated Hanisch and contributed to the acrimonious breakup of their partnership in 1911.

By then, Hitler had branched out from postcards into larger works aimed at Vienna's two biggest markets for cheap paintings: frame makers, who customarily sold their wares complete with pictures, and furniture manufacturers who made a popular style of sofa with a painting set into the upholstery on the back. Hitler worked steadily as a supplier to these branches of the interior-decorating trade until 1913, when he moved to Munich to escape service in the Austrian army. There he sold his paintings door-to-door and rendered dozens of pictures of the local registry office, selling them as souvenirs to newlywed couples as they emerged from the building. Hitler's career as a professional artist ended with the war, but he continued to draw and paint while in the army, recording his battlefront impressions with numerous sketches and watercolors.

Hitler was unaffected by the currents of modernism sweeping the art world in the early twentieth century, and he worked in a rigidly conservative style. Because of his interest in architecture, he specialized in street scenes, often copied from other pictures. Except for human figures, which he drew poorly, the results were competent if uninspired. An art critic who was once asked to comment on Hitler's work without being told his identity pronounced the paintings "quite good" on the whole. The expert noted, however, that the cartoonish human figures betrayed a fundamental "disinterest in people."

A Range of Early Expressions

Hitler's caricature of one of his secondary-school instructors, done when the artist was about thirteen, graphically conveys his contempt for teachers.

In 1901, twelve-year-old Adolf sketched this helmeted medieval warrior, probably copying the picture out of a book.

Hitler included this bucolic ▷ watercolor in the portfolio he submitted to Vienna's Academy of Fine Arts when he applied there for admission in 1907.

As an eighteenth birthday gift to his friend Gustl Kubizek, Hitler drew up plans (above and right) for "Villa Gustl," a Renaissance-style palazzo he promised to build one day.

A Penchant for Buildings

Hitler apparently used an old lithograph as the source for this drawing of the domed eighteenth-century Hofburg and the neighboring Burgtheater.

A watercolor of one of Hitler's favorite subjects, the Parliament building, overlooking Vienna's Ringstrasse, shows his facility for architectural drawing.

Hitler's awkward and poorly drawn human figures add a clumsy note to a circa 1911 painting of the Scots' Gate, a medieval Viennese landmark.

The *Ratzenstadl*, or Rats' Town, was a crowded, poor quarter of Vienna until it was cleaned up in the nineteenth century. Here Hitler depicts the neighborhood in its refurbished state.

This 1914 watercolor depicts a shelter dug into the bank of a sunken lane near the Flemish town of Wychaete.

Hitler painted this view of Haubourdin, a village outside Lille, France, in 1916. He was billeted there for several months in a butcher shop.

A 1916 pencil portrait of an infantryman shows the new steel helmet introduced into the German army that year.

Hitler's watercolor of Becelaere, on the Belgian front, shows the shell damage done to the town and its Gothic church.

Selections from a Soldier's Sketchbook

"On to Comines!" scrawled Hitler across a pen-and-ink sketch of his platoon marching along a muddy road in Flanders. Each man is identified by name; Hitler is third from the left.

VOLK und ZEIT

EIN ERSTES HOCH
AUF DIE JUNGE
DEUTSCHE REPUBLIK

THREE

The Foredoomed Republic

he revolutionary passions sweeping Germany mounted to fever pitch on Saturday, November 9, 1918. The abdication of Emperor William II had just been announced, and in Berlin the citizenry danced in the streets. Carousing soldiers refused to obey their officers and fired rifles into the air; even elite Prussian units, rushed to the capital because of their presumed loyalty, refused to use arms to restore order. Workers called a general strike and marched by the thousands toward the center of the capital, waving the blood-red banner of bolshevism. "The only masters of Berlin," an army officer wrote later, "were Disunity, Licentiousness, and Chaos."

Inside the seat of national government, however, an orderly if unconventional transition was taking place. A few minutes after the decision was made for the kaiser to step down, a delegation of Reichstag members arrived at the chancellery. In a brief meeting, the chancellor, Prince Max of Baden, lacking constitutional authorization but acting sensibly to meet the crisis, handed over his office to Friedrich Ebert, leader of the Social Democratic party. Ebert, for his part, promised to govern in accordance with the existing constitution and to convene a constituent assembly to consider what form Germany's postwar government should take.

The forty-seven-year-old Ebert was no radical despite his Socialist label. The son of a Heidelberg tailor and himself a one-time saddler and saloon keeper, Ebert looked more like a modest businessman than a political power. Yet he was a skilled negotiator, an ardent patriot, and a partisan of the monarchy, for which two of his sons had died during the war. In fact, he still hoped to establish a constitutional monarchy like the British system, perhaps with one of the kaiser's six sons serving as regent. Such a system, he believed, was the only alternative to revolution, which he abhorred. "I want no part of it," he had said recently. "I hate it as I hate sin."

But the force of revolutionary fervor proved more powerful than Ebert's intentions. As the new chancellor and his colleagues were having a meager lunch of watery soup in the Reichstag dining hall that afternoon, a group of soldiers and workers burst in. The intruders implored Ebert's deputy, Philipp Scheidemann, the party's best-known orator, to speak to the

Hats and fists aloft, participants in the November revolution of 1918 hail the birth of the Weimar Republic and the end of four draining years of war. On the tenth anniversary of the revolt, this picture appeared on the cover of the German magazine *Volk und Zeit* (People and time).

crowds massed outside. At the imperial palace a few blocks away, they said, Marxists had gained control and were about to proclaim a Soviet regime. That was enough for Scheidemann, who, like Ebert, loathed bolshevism.

Hoping to harness this runaway revolution before the Bolsheviks could prevail, Scheidemann rushed to a window overlooking the Königsplatz and stuck his head out. To the cheers of the multitudes below him, he spoke briefly of the end of the war, the kaiser's announced abdication, and the selection of Ebert as chancellor. Then, galvanized by the groundswell of emotion, he cried out, "Long live the new! Long live the German republic!" Ebert was appalled. "You have no right!" he roared. "The fate of Germany must be decided by a constituent assembly." But it was too late. Scheidemann had pronounced the death of nearly a half-century of empire and the birth of a republic. There was no turning back.

After he had recovered from the shock, Ebert formed a six-man provisional council to govern the new republic pending the election of the constituent assembly. This cabinet-like group included Ebert, Scheidemann, and a third Social Democrat, together with three of Ebert's former colleagues now in the Independent Socialist party. The Independent Socialists, who had split from the Social Democrats two years before in opposition to the war, were far more radical than Ebert and his colleagues; they favored immediate socialization of heavy industry and empowerment of the soldiers' and workers' councils springing up all over the nation.

Those philosophical conflicts aside, the government of the new republic faced enormous obstacles. It had to restore order, revive an economy on the verge of collapse, feed a nation slowly being starved to death by the Allied blockade, and negotiate a peace settlement. Moreover, Germany's new leaders somehow had to implant and nourish the concept of political democracy. The German people not only lacked experience in its practice but also had a distaste for the necessary partisan give-and-take—for what Thomas Mann derided as the "virus of politics." Although the monarchy had been swept away, the old attitudes and the institutions that underlay it remained firmly in place: the imperial army, the government bureaucracy, the Junker landlords east of the Elbe, and the industrialists of the Ruhr. Someone would aptly refer later to "this revolution without revolutionaries" that "produced a republic with few republicans."

The nature of the problems facing Ebert was dramatically illustrated by the government's first order of business: officially ending the war. At five o'clock on the morning of November 11, two days after the birth of the republic, a German civilian representative, Matthias Erzberger, signed an armistice agreement with the Allies in a railroad car in the French Forest of Compiègne. Six hours later, the guns fell silent.

While dejected aides pace around him, Emperor William II *(at center, wearing a fur collar)* **waits at the Belgian border on the morning of November 10, 1918, for the train that will take him into lifelong exile.**

By signing the document, the new republic became a symbol of despair, defeat, and humiliation. The German high command escaped odium because its army was largely intact at the time of the truce, the Allies having delivered no single decisive blow. Moreover, Woodrow Wilson, the American president, had refused to deal with what he termed the "military masters" of Germany. These circumstances would allow a dangerous fantasy to take root: that the army had not been defeated in the field but had been stabbed in the back by "subversive" elements at home—pacifists, liberals, Communists, Jews, and socialists responsible for the new republic.

Field Marshal Paul von Hindenburg was a foremost exponent of the myth. "Like Siegfried, stricken down by the treacherous spear of the savage Hagen, our weary front collapsed," he wrote. And he later testified: "In spite of the superiority of the enemy in men and matériel, we could have brought the struggle to a favorable issue if determined and unanimous cooperation had existed between the army and those at home."

Indeed, Chancellor Ebert himself had helped propagate the fiction of German invincibility. On the morning of December 11, the legions returning from France and Belgium had marched up the Unter den Linden, rifles on their shoulders, flags flying and bands playing. At the Brandenburg Gate, surmounted by its chariot of victory, Ebert had proudly welcomed them home with the words: "I salute you, who return unvanquished from the field of battle." The chancellor meant simply to honor and gratify the troops. But his words had effectively absolved the general staff of responsibility for defeat and condemned his own revolutionary republic. Before long, Germany would see a powerful resurgence of the militarism that had just ended in debacle.

From the very start, Ebert had worried far more about the threat from the Left than from the Right. He and his colleagues were haunted by the recent Bolshevik revolution in Russia, where soldiers' and workers' councils like those now mushrooming throughout Germany had seized power. He feared that the radical wing of the Independent Socialists or, worse, the Marxists of the Spartacus League would seize control of the councils and challenge the government. The resulting violence might topple the repub-

Defeated German soldiers assume a posture of victory as they parade through Berlin's Brandenburg Gate (*above, left*) on December 11, 1918. With bands playing and spectators cheering from the treetops (*above, right*), the idea took hold that they had been not beaten but betrayed.

lic or even bring military intervention by the intently watching Allies.

To preserve order, Ebert had concluded a secret alliance with the Supreme Command of the Imperial Army. The pact was negotiated on the evening of November 9, after his first tumultuous day in office. Ebert was pacing in his office in the chancellery, listening to the boisterous demonstrators outside and pondering his melancholy prospects, when a desk telephone rang. The line was a special one connecting the chancellery with army headquarters at Spa in Belgium. The voice was that of Hindenburg's new deputy, General Wilhelm Groener, who earlier that day had helped

force the kaiser's decision to abdicate by bluntly informing his emperor that he no longer commanded the loyalty of the army. Now, shrewdly, Groener wanted to strike a bargain with the nascent republic. It was quickly done—and confirmed by telegram from Berlin to Spa. In exchange for Ebert's promise to combat bolshevism and preserve the traditional officers' corps, Groener pledged the support of the supreme command in maintaining order. "From then on," wrote Groener later, "we discussed the measures that were necessary every evening on the secret telephone line."

Ebert's pact with the general staff was soon put to the test. In mid-December, a national congress of elected representatives was convened in Berlin. Although Ebert's Social Democrats dominated the congress, rejecting radical demands for a proletarian dictatorship, deep-seated antagonisms against the old army were too powerful to resist. Despite Ebert's opposition, the delegates overwhelmingly approved resolutions to dismiss the supreme commander, reduce the power of the officers' corps, and even abolish the regular army. They wanted to replace it with a so-called *Freiwillige Volkswehr,* or volunteer people's militia, in which all insignia of rank would be eliminated and the soldiers would elect their own officers.

Under his bargain with the generals, Ebert could only ignore the radical resolutions. Hindenburg left him no room for maneuver. "You may tell Herr Ebert," said the field marshal to Groener, "that I decline to recognize the ruling of the congress with regard to the executive authority of our officers; that I shall oppose it by every means in my power; and that I shall not allow my epaulets or my sword to be taken from me. The army supports the government and expects it to carry out its promise to preserve the army."

Ebert's inaction infuriated his cabinet partners, the Independent Socialists, who immediately started to stir up the soldiers' councils in Berlin. One notorious affiliate of the councils was a group of ill-disciplined sailors known as the People's Naval Division. These men had occupied the imperial palace and stables since the early days of the revolution, ostensibly protecting the republic while helping themselves to the wine cellars and installing girlfriends in royal luxury.

When the sailors demanded 125,000 marks to leave the palace, Ebert paid the ransom. They demanded 80,000 marks more, and when he refused, they erupted in anger. On December 23, the sailors surrounded Ebert's chancellery, severed telephone communications, and seized several city officials as hostages. The one line the rebels failed to cut was Ebert's secret connection to the supreme command, now in the German city of Kassel. Ebert picked up the phone and appealed for the army's help.

Early the next morning, Christmas Eve, a small division of about 800 Prussian Horse Guards equipped with light artillery marched in from

Friedrich Ebert strides into an uncertain future after his appointment as provisional president of Germany in February 1919. A former harness maker, Ebert was unequal to the challenges facing the new German republic.

Potsdam. By that time, the government had reached a compromise with the 1,200 mutinous sailors, who had retired to the grounds of the palace. Even so, the order was passed down for the Horse Guards to take on the radical rebels, and they opened fire. After two hours of fighting, the beleaguered sailors were ready to surrender. But at that moment, a hostile mob of civilians swarmed into the square and surrounded the soldiers, throwing them into confusion. Rather than fire into the crowd, which included women and children, the once-proud Prussian guards dropped their weapons and ran away.

The humiliation of Christmas Eve led to an even closer alliance between the officers' corps and the Ebert government. Five days later, the Independent Socialists resigned from Ebert's government, to be replaced immediately by members of Ebert's party. Most notable among them was Ebert's old friend and Reichstag colleague, Gustav Noske, who was named defense minister and charged with raising a force capable of protecting the embattled government.

Noske had a reputation, rare among Social Democrats, as a hard-liner in matters of national security. A former butcher and noncommissioned officer in the imperial army, he became the party's specialist on military affairs not long after his election to the Reichstag in 1906. As Prince Max's military governor in Kiel during the last days of the monarchy, his handling of the sailors' mutiny there had won him the admiration of the officers' corps. Compact and strongly built, he made no apologies for the use of force. "Somebody will have to be the bloodhound," he said at his first cabinet meeting. "I will not shirk the responsibility."

The new minister never doubted that he would have to rely on the officers' corps for the force necessary to maintain order. But the source of the troops that would be needed was a problem. The Christmas Eve calamity had demonstrated the unsuitability of the two most obvious pools

An artillery shell slams into the imperial stables in Berlin, the redoubt of a rebellious 600-man naval unit, during an attack by government forces in December of 1918. The sailors had come to Berlin to defend the young republic but stayed on to pillage and carouse.

Shocked citizens survey the rubble left by the battle to clear the imperial palace and stables of unruly sailors. After a lengthy exchange of gunfire on Christmas Eve, remnants of the once-proud German army gave up the fight, demonstrating their inability to maintain order.

of manpower—the militia units that represented the soldiers' and sailors' councils, and what remained of the army itself. The militia outfits were as likely to be enemies as allies. And the heavily conscripted army had largely dissolved since returning home in December. The ranks were so depleted by the last days of 1918 that, in all of Berlin, the army could count on no more than 150 effective regular troops to guard the seat of government.

There was a third alternative, however. Early in the new year, on January 4, 1919, Noske and Ebert drove to the army's Camp Zossen on the outskirts of Berlin. There, on the frozen parade ground, they reviewed Maercker's Volunteer Rifles, a force of 4,000 well-equipped men who marched past in perfect formation. This unit, named for its founder, General Ludwig von Maercker, was one of the first of a remarkable new kind of military organization known as the *Freikorps*, or Free Corps.

The Freikorps were highly disciplined units of volunteers raised from the ruins of the old army. Maercker, former commander of the 214th Infantry Division, had put his outfit together in only three weeks after winning approval from the supreme command in early December. The supreme command paid, fed, uniformed, and equipped Maercker's men, and it encouraged other officers to follow his example. Drawn from the ranks of demobilized soldiers, fanatical nationalists, military adventurers, and unemployed youths, new units ranging in size from a mere handful of men to nearly a regiment were rapidly organizing all over Germany.

Typically, a junior officer or even a sergeant from the regular army took the initiative in raising such a group and gave it his name. Under the so-called *Führer* principle, taken from the prewar youth movement and enshrined among elite storm troops during the war, Freikorps leaders

demanded unquestioning, unwavering obedience from the ranks. The men called their commander the Führer and idolized him as the embodiment of all soldierly virtues.

Few recruits signed up with a Freikorps out of allegiance to the new republic. All of the officers and most of the men detested it, in fact. When a journalist asked Colonel Wilhelm Reinhardt, one of the first Freikorps commanders, if it was true that he had called the government a rabble and its black, red, and gold flag a Jewish rag, he cheerfully admitted that he had. "I make no bones about the fact that I am a monarchist. My God! When one has served his king and his country faithfully for thirty years, one can't suddenly say, 'Starting tomorrow, I'm a republican.'"

More than monarchy, the soldiers of the Freikorps glorified nationalism and militarism and manifested a bleak hostility toward communism, socialism, democracy, and Jews. Proud of their nihilism, they referred to themselves as *Landsknechte*—"Freebooters." These were the men who would later form the spearhead of forces seeking to undermine and destroy the republic. Indeed, nearly half of the Nazi party leadership would come from veterans of the Freikorps.

Yet none of this was apparent to Gustav Noske that day on the parade ground at Zossen. He needed these troops, and they had flattered him: Never before had the army accorded mere civilians full military honors by marching in review before them. "You can relax now," Noske told Ebert as they drove back to Berlin. "Everything will be all right." Two days later, the government officially recognized the Freikorps and appealed to all able-bodied German males to offer themselves as recruits. By mid-May, there would be 400,000 men under arms. The phoenix had risen.

For Noske, the protectors of the republic had materialized in the nick of time. Turmoil gripped Berlin, and with elections for the constituent assembly less than two weeks away, the capital appeared vulnerable to a Bolshevik takeover. Much of the trouble was brewed by the far-left radicals of the Spartacus League, who took their name from the ancient Roman gladiator and leader of a slave revolt. Inspired by the Russian example, the Spartacists wanted a sovietized Germany. At a year-end congress in Berlin, they had formally broken their last ties with the Independent Socialists and reconstituted themselves as the Communist party of Germany.

While firm in their purpose, the party's two leaders were divided in their ideas about tactics. Karl Liebknecht, whose father, Wilhelm, had been one of the founders of the Social Democratic party, favored an immediate armed takeover. But Rosa Luxemburg, the brilliant Polish-born Marxist theoretician, counseled prudence. She felt that the party was still too weak;

better to build mass support, even participate in the upcoming national elections. But the militant congress brushed all that aside; the delegates voted to boycott the elections and roared for immediate action.

The opportunity came less than a week later. On January 4—the same day Noske and Ebert reviewed Maercker's Freikorps—the government dismissed the police chief of Berlin, Emil Eichhorn, an Independent Socialist whose sympathies lay with the Left. Denouncing the "tyranny of Ebert," the Communists joined with the Independent Socialists in a call for massive demonstrations—and within a few days the demonstrations led to fighting with the Freikorps. Rushing in from their camps outside Berlin, Maercker's Volunteer Rifles and other units responded to the emergency with a brutal relish that was to become their trademark. It was all over in Berlin by January 17, the Communists savagely put down, their leaders, Liebknecht and Luxemburg, captured and murdered in cold blood.

Although Ebert and his colleagues "very likely got more than they bargained for," as a British newspaper correspondent described it, the suppression of the Berlin Bolsheviks achieved the government's immediate goal: trouble-free elections for the constituent assembly on January 19. More than 80 percent of the electorate, including women for the first time, went to the polls and gave a heartening vote of confidence to Germany's fragile democracy. About 75 percent of the ballots went to candidates of the three moderate parties that backed the republic: the Social Democrats, the Democrats, and the Catholic Center party.

Berlin still seethed with such radicalism, however, that Ebert transferred the National Assembly to Weimar, 150 miles southwest of the capital. A small, relatively isolated city much easier to defend than Berlin, this shrine of German liberalism and home of the great poets Goethe and Schiller thus gave its name to what history would know as the Weimar Republic. Convening on February 6 within the steel ring of 7,000 troops from Maercker's Volunteer Rifles, the assembly immediately elected Ebert the first president of Germany. He then selected his old comrade Philipp Scheidemann as chancellor and, since the 38 percent of the popular vote accorded the Social Democrats fell short of a majority, authorized him to form a coalition cabinet with the Democrats and the Centrists.

While the assembly began the laborious process of drafting a new constitution, pockets of rebellion flared up all through the winter and spring of 1919. In cities across Germany, from Bremen to Munich, from Mülheim to Dresden, the Communists and their allies attempted to undermine the proceedings in Weimar by calling general strikes and proclaiming local Soviet republics. Noske, in his function as bloodhound, responded by dispatching the fearsome troubleshooters of the Freikorps to restore order.

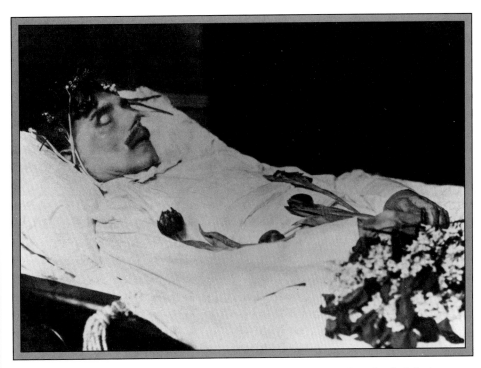

At left, Rosa Luxemburg, a principal leader of the German Communist party, promenades on a Berlin street. In January 1919, Freikorps soldiers shot Luxemburg and dumped her body into a Berlin canal.

Rosa Luxemburg's associate Karl Liebknecht (right) was arrested during preelection fighting between the German Communists and the right-wing Freikorps—then beaten and shot to death.

The Freebooters gloried in these opportunities for a battle. "Fighting was the whole content and meaning of their lives," wrote Heinz Oskar Hauenstein, a young noncommissioned officer who formed his own unit of volunteers. "Nothing else made any sense. It was battle alone that they loved. The battle that was hard, brutal, pitiless."

The bloodiest outbreak began on March 3 in Berlin, where resurgent Communists stormed thirty-two police stations in the eastern part of the city. Against some 15,000 rebels, Noske concentrated 42,000 Freikorps troops supported by artillery, flamethrowers, and even tanks. The rebels were driven into the Lichtenberg suburbs, and the fighting slackened. But then, reports of atrocities against the Lichtenberg police, erroneous, as it happened, prompted Noske to issue an order on March 9 to shoot on the spot "any person who bears arms against government troops." With this hunting license, the Freebooters ran wild, lashing out indiscriminately for four days. When the fury finally abated, nearly 1,500 people—innocent bystanders among them—lay dead.

In early May, after Freikorps units suppressed a Red regime in Munich and imposed their own "White Terror," an exhausted calm settled over Germany. Only five months before, the leaders of the republic had felt unsafe even in their own offices. Now, thanks to the ruthless efficiency of the Freikorps, the nation, for the time being at least, had been pacified.

As the menace of domestic disorder subsided, a new crisis confronted the German republic. Delegates of the victorious Allied powers had been meeting in Paris since January to draft a permanent peace settlement. The Germans expected to pay a stern price for losing the war, though not a crushing one. To begin with, few among them felt a sense of responsibility for starting the war. In any event, the country had repudiated the wartime monarchy and had reconstituted itself as a Western-style democracy. Encouraged by their leaders, Germans anticipated a peace treaty rooted in the spirit of reconciliation endorsed by President Wilson in his famous

Fourteen Points speech of 1917. Indeed, it was widely believed that Germany had voluntarily laid down its arms in response—if somewhat belated—to Wilson's proposals, and one South German town had greeted its returning troops with banners inscribed: "Welcome, brave soldiers, your work has been done: God and Wilson will carry it on."

It is little wonder that Germany reacted with shock and dismay on May 7 when the Allies presented their draft of the Treaty of Versailles. Its terms, beginning with the military, seemed aimed at reducing a proud nation to third-class status. The treaty limited the army to a volunteer force of merely 4,000 officers and 96,000 men with no organized reserve. It banned all aircraft, tanks, and other offensive weapons and eliminated such bulwarks of German military tradition as the general staff, the war academy, and the cadet schools. At the same time, the German navy was to be limited to 15,000 officers and men with a token fleet of mainly patrol vessels, the largest of which could not exceed 10,000 tons; there would be no submarines. Allied inspectors would roam the Reich supervising the destruction of existing arms and enforcing the treaty limits.

The terms also bit deeply into Germany's geographical and physical resources. In addition to forfeiting all of its colonies in Africa and elsewhere, the nation would be forced to surrender 13 percent of the prewar homeland and some six million people. In the west, the provinces of Alsace and Lorraine would revert to France, from which they had been taken in 1871. Smaller border parcels would go to Belgium and Denmark. The German region west of the Rhine, known as the Rhineland, would be occupied by the Allies for up to fifteen years. This area and a strip thirty miles wide east of the Rhine would be permanently demilitarized. In the east, the industrially rich region of Upper Silesia was to be ceded to the new nation of Poland. Even more importantly, Poland would receive a great part of the provinces of Posen and West Prussia. The latter would provide the new Polish Corridor to the Baltic Sea and would separate Germany from East Prussia, which was left isolated on the far side of Poland. These losses could not be offset by annexation of Austria. Such a union, though favored by both countries, was forbidden under the treaty.

Other terms of the treaty targeted Germany's economy. One provision would eliminate most of its merchant marine fleet. Another would further cripple its international trade by giving the victorious powers most-favored nation treatment in Germany for five years while effectively barring German goods from Allied markets. The Saar Basin, source of much of Germany's

Freikorps soldiers on a balcony overlooking the Brandenburg Gate train a machine gun on the Unter den Linden. More than 1,000 people were killed in the street-fighting of March 1919, and martial law remained in force until the end of the year.

coal, was to be placed under control of the new League of Nations for fifteen years, at the end of which time a plebiscite would decide its future. Meanwhile, the French would operate the mines to compensate for the destruction of their own during the war. Germany would also have to pay for the damage it had inflicted upon other nations during the fighting. Since the Allies could not agree on the precise amount, which promised to be enormous, these reparations were to be determined later.

For all of the military, territorial, and commercial punishment inflicted upon the new republic, it was the so-called points of honor that were the most galling. These provisions, embodied in Articles 227 through 231, assessed the blame for the war. Emperor William II and other leaders were to be handed over to foreign tribunals for trial on charges of violating the laws of war. To justify the Allied claim to reparations, Article 231 required that Germany confess sole responsibility for causing World War I.

Germans of every stripe reacted with disbelief and rage. President Ebert called the proposed settlement a "peace of violence." The Scheidemann cabinet labeled the terms "unfulfillable, unfeasible, and ruinous for Germany." Theaters and other places of public entertainment shut down, and people gathered everywhere in spontaneous protest.

The German government had two weeks in which to state its objections and counterproposals—in writing, for the Allies permitted no oral discussion. The resulting German document turned out to be nearly twice as long as the treaty itself, filling 443 pages. All the complaints brought only one significant concession: Rather than stipulating the outright cession of Upper Silesia to the Poles, the treaty instead would allow a plebiscite to determine the region's future. (As it turned out, Germany won the plebiscite in 1921 but lost the richest part of Upper Silesia anyway.)

The Allies refused to budge on the other issues, and it was now clear that a rejection of the treaty would almost certainly bring a renewal of the war. On June 22, the National Assembly agreed to ratify the treaty, but still repudiated the points of honor—the five articles dealing with war criminals and war guilt. The Allies were adamant: Ratify or reject the entire treaty before 6:00 p.m. the following day, June 23. "The time for discussion has passed," declared France's premier, Georges Clemenceau.

President Ebert was inclined to reject such draconian terms, come what might, and only the pleadings of his colleagues prevented him from resigning. His strongman in the defense ministry, Gustav Noske, was vacillating. Noske had been approached by a group of top generals who were so stridently against signing that they were willing to risk giving up western Germany and fighting the Allies from the old Prussian provinces in the east. The generals implored Noske to take over the government and establish a

At Versailles, the Allies forced the Weimar Republic to make painful territorial concessions (*dark green*). Alsace-Lorraine was returned to France, North Schleswig given to Denmark. The Baltic port of Memel and its surrounding area went to Lithuania. Upper Silesia and a large section of Prussia was ceded to Poland, separating historic East Prussia from the rest of the fatherland. Hitler and the Nazis castigated Germany's new democratic government for signing the so-called Treaty of Shame, which had shrunk the nation's borders (*red line*).

A Diminished Germany

military dictatorship. Noske, evidently flirting with this fantasy, announced his intention to resign from the government.

It was nearly noon, with the Allied deadline little more than six hours away, when Ebert rang up his contact at the supreme command, General Groener. What were the chances, Ebert asked, of mounting a successful defense against an Allied invasion if the treaty were rejected?

It was a question the general staff had been debating for days. The Freikorps leader Wilhelm Reinhardt had urged defiance and renewed war. Old Hindenburg had proclaimed that he far preferred "to perish honorably than to accept a shameful peace." Hindenburg had asked Groener: "Should we not appeal to the corps of officers and demand from a minority of the people a gesture of sacrifice in defense of our national honor?" Groener had replied flatly that "such a gesture would be lost on the German people. There would be a general outcry against counterrevolution and militarism. The result would only be the downfall of the Reich. The Allies would show themselves pitiless. The officers' corps would be destroyed, and the name of Germany would disappear from the map."

With blunt honesty, Groener had counseled capitulation, and he now

answered Ebert in the same way. Speaking "as a German" rather than as a general, Groener advised that armed resistance was hopeless. Germany had no choice but to accept the hateful treaty.

Ebert now moved swiftly to accept the inevitable. At Groener's suggestion, he asked Noske to withdraw his resignation and appeal to the army to stand by the government. Noske agreed, and the cabinet approved ratification of the treaty. In the National Assembly, proponents of acceptance extracted agreement from the die-hards on condition that it be known that patriotism alone impelled their support. Only then did Germany's elected representatives accept the Treaty of Versailles.

Official notification reached the Allies just nineteen minutes before their ultimatum expired. Five days later, on June 28, the official signing took place in the Hall of Mirrors at Versailles—the same splendid venue where, nearly a half-century previously, William I of Prussia had celebrated victory over France and proclaimed the new German Empire.

The peace settlement and the subsequent lifting of the Allied blockade enabled the National Assembly to return to the task that previously had occupied its energy. The lawmakers completed the new Weimar constitution and overwhelmingly approved the document on July 31, five weeks after the ceremony at Versailles. The constitution formally established a democratic republic far more centralized than the old monarchy. Prerogatives such as taxation and control of the military that had been vested in the individual *Länder*, or states, now resided in a central government headed by a president. Elected directly by the people for a seven-year term, the president managed foreign affairs, commanded the military, and appointed the chancellor. There was to be a bicameral legislature: an appointive upper house, or Reichsrat, representing the interests of the eighteen states, and a popularly elected lower house, or Reichstag, which confirmed the chancellor and his cabinet and approved all legislation.

There were two contrasting provisions of the constitution, however, that would have fateful consequences for the republic. To ensure that all shades of opinion found expression in the Reichstag, the election of members was based on proportional representation, which allotted seats to a party in accordance with its popular vote. This fostered a proliferation of small parties, making it virtually impossible for any single party to command a majority. The result was a bewildering succession of coalition governments so ineffectual that they undermined public respect for democracy.

A second critical provision—Article 48—allowed arbitrary rule by the chief of state. "Should public order and safety be seriously disturbed or threatened," read the article, the president could employ the armed forces,

rule by decree, even suspend freedom of speech and other guaranteed liberties. Framers of the constitution undoubtedly had in mind the anarchic early months of the republic when they drafted Article 48, but its repeated use would later contribute to the demise of German democracy.

The democracy was already under public assault for its acceptance of the vindictive Versailles treaty. Widespread feelings of humiliation turned into bitter criticism of the government and the *Diktat*, or dictated peace. Ebert tried to defuse the protests by winning small concessions. In February 1920, the Allies agreed to allow alleged war criminals to be tried in Germany instead of abroad. The Dutch, who had given the emperor refuge, refused to extradite him, and he was never brought to trial. Of the original Allied list of 895 suspects, only 12 were actually tried and 6 convicted—but that was small comfort, and the chorus of discontent grew louder.

The government returned to Berlin from Weimar in September 1919, and at the turn of the year it was clear that threats to its survival had shifted from the Communists to the radical right. The greatest potential menace resided in President Ebert's old ally, the army, which had incorporated the best of the Freikorps units and had been renamed the *Reichswehr*, for "state defense." Ebert's personal link to the officers' corps, General Groener, was gone, hounded into retirement by the growing myth that the army once again had been stabbed in the back.

The ranks of Freebooters seethed with grievances. During the summer of 1919, the Ebert government, acting at the behest of the Allies, had ordered several Freikorps units home from the Baltic region, where they had been fighting Russian Communists and local nationalists since February. The recall order deprived them of territorial gains achieved in Latvia and Lithuania, thus puncturing their dream of using the Baltic states as a base from which to overthrow the republic. Then, early in 1920, fresh anger gripped the Freebooters as the government, complying with treaty provisions to reduce the Reichswehr to 100,000 officers and men, began to slash the ranks of the Freikorps at a time of widespread unemployment.

By that time, a conspiracy to bring down the republic was taking shape. Its military leader was General Walther von Lüttwitz, who as overall commander of Berlin troops had suppressed the Spartacist uprising in January 1919. An able soldier and a Prussian aristocrat, the sixty-one-year-old Lüttwitz venerated the monarchy and wanted nothing so much as its restoration. His sixty-two-year-old civilian counterpart, Dr. Wolfgang Kapp, had been born and raised in America but had absorbed little of democracy from his birthplace or from his father, a distinguished German liberal who had been forced into exile in New York after the revolution of 1848. Upon his return to Germany, the younger Kapp had served as a bureaucrat in East

In a 1919 cartoon *(above)*, a victorious Freikorps officer amid a litter of corpses toasts Defense Minister Gustav Noske, who directed the bloody repression of the Communist uprisings. In the photograph at right, Noske *(far right)* consults with General Lüttwitz, commander of the First Army District in Berlin.

115

Prussia and had devoted himself enthusiastically to causes of the far right.

The catalyst for what became the Kapp Putsch occurred in late February 1920. The government, acting on its treaty obligation to reduce Germany's military forces, attempted to disband two units under Lüttwitz's command. One of them was the notorious 2d Marine Brigade, under Lieutenant Commander Hermann Ehrhardt, whom subordinates described as a leader of primitive directness. The brigade had spearheaded the suppression of the Communist revolt in Bavaria the previous May and then fought Polish nationalists in Upper Silesia, where the unit recruited hundreds of battle-hardened veterans of the Baltic Freikorps. Now billeted at Camp Döberitz, near Berlin, the 5,000 men in the Ehrhardt Brigade were outraged at the very notion of disbanding.

General Lüttwitz quickly capitalized on their discontent, publicly assuring them that he would permit no demobilization. The general's blatant insubordination, amid rumors of a coup, convinced Noske to fire him and order Kapp's arrest. But it was too late. Forewarned, the conspirators went into hiding, and Lüttwitz set the putsch in motion.

On Friday evening, March 12, renewed reports of impending trouble led Noske to dispatch his naval commander, Admiral Adolf von Trotha, to Camp Döberitz to check on the Ehrhardt Brigade. Trotha was not a good choice. Rebellious himself, he telephoned ahead to Camp Döberitz to warn the brigade of his coming and thus found everything quite correct upon his arrival. Trotha returned to Berlin about ten o'clock and reported "all quiet." An hour later, the Ehrhardt Brigade was on the march to Berlin.

Around midnight, Noske learned of their advance from a newspaper reporter. He sent two generals to intercept Ehrhardt, futilely hoping to reason with the man. In the small hours of the morning, Noske called a meeting of his top military leaders and asked them what measures should be taken against the rebels. The old alliance between republic and army was on the line—and to Noske's dismay, it soon became clear that many of the generals who had willingly stamped out leftist uprisings had no stomach for quashing one from the Right. As General Hans von Seeckt, the Prussian aristocrat who served as the Reichswehr's military chief, put it: "Troops do not fire on troops. Do you perhaps intend, Herr Minister, that a battle be fought before the Brandenburg Gate between troops who have fought side by side against the common enemy? When Reichswehr fires on Reichswehr, then all comradeship with the officers' corps has vanished."

Noske and Ebert had little choice. At five o'clock in the morning, they and the cabinet fled Berlin by automobile, moving the seat of government to Dresden and then, eventually, to Stuttgart to carry on the struggle.

The government had scarcely departed when, at seven o'clock on that

The very model of a Prussian officer, General Hans von Seeckt is photographed at about the time he became commander in chief of the German army. Asked about the army's sympathies, he replied, "I do not know if it is reliable, but it obeys me."

Saturday morning, the Ehrhardt Brigade marched through the Brandenburg Gate into central Berlin. The flag-bearers held aloft the black, white, and red banner of imperial Germany, and the men wore emblazoned upon their steel helmets the swastika that one day would become synonymous with nazism. They were welcomed by the city's police, by General Lüttwitz, and by Wolfgang Kapp at the head of an array of civilian dignitaries in morning dress complete with top hats and spats.

The group included General Erich Ludendorff, Groener's predecessor

and the man who had virtually ruled Germany during the last two years of the war. Ludendorff hovered in the background of the Kapp conspiracy, later insisting that he merely happened to be out for a morning walk when he saw the commotion. In any event, he and the others proceeded to march at the head of Ehrhardt's troops to Wilhelmstrasse, where the putschists took over the government without a single shot being fired.

Kapp was proclaimed chancellor but was hardly prepared to govern. He later asserted that he had not even known of the march until that very morning. Certainly he evidenced no plan of action. Typical of the comic-opera debut of his regime was the experience of his wife, who was to have written the new administration's manifesto to the people. She could not

The 2,500-man Ehrhardt Brigade strides into Berlin *(above)* on March 13, 1920, determined to overthrow the Weimar government, which had tried to disband all Freikorps units as required by the Versailles treaty. On arrival, the rebels unfurled the flag of the German monarchy *(right)* and proclaimed Dr. Wolfgang Kapp chancellor.

find a typewriter upon her arrival at the chancellery. By the time one was procured it was too late to make the Sunday newspapers, and most Germans remained unaware of the coup until Monday.

Kapp likewise was unprepared for the hostile reception accorded his upstart regime by the bureaucracy. Most government officials refused to obey his orders. The treasury balked at paying his troops, and when Kapp suggested that Ehrhardt take the money by force, the Freebooter replied icily that he was not, after all, a bank robber. More inhospitable still were Berlin's workers. Even as the government fled the capital, a proclamation calling for a general strike had been issued in the name of Ebert and the Social Democrats. "Workers, Comrades!" cried the manifesto. "The military putsch is under way. We did not raise the revolution in order to acknowledge once again the bloody rule of mercenaries. We will make no deal with the Baltic criminals. Strike, stop working, strangle this military dictatorship. Fight, forget all dissension! Cripple the country's economic life! Not a hand must move. General strike all along the line. Workers unite!"

The strike was full-blown by midafternoon on the following day, Sunday, March 14. It was one of the most effective walkouts in history. Berlin came to a complete standstill—all commerce, all industry, all services ended; there was no transport, no electricity, not even any water.

By March 17, Kapp was at his wits' end. He shunned counsel to break the strike by firing on the strikers, and then saw rebellion infect army units garrisoned in Berlin. Heretofore neutral, these troops suddenly started arresting their officers and calling for an end to the putsch. Demands for Kapp's resignation now came from the police and other one-time sympathizers. Before noon, Kapp gave it up and, naming Lüttwitz as his successor, fled to Sweden. A few hours later, Lüttwitz also resigned.

As the Ehrhardt Brigade marched out of the capital that afternoon, a crowd lined the Unter den Linden, staring in angry silence. The sailors were in an ugly mood. When a small boy laughed, two of them broke ranks and clubbed him to the ground with their rifle butts and then kicked his prostrate body. "No one dared interfere," recalled an Englishman who was there, "but the crowd hissed. At that, an officer shouted some words of command. The troops opened fire. The street suddenly resounded with the *rat-tat* of machine guns, the whistling of bullets, the crack of splintered glass, and the cries and groans of the wounded. The people ran. The rest lay where they had fallen. Then came another command—to cease fire— followed by 'Quick march!' "

A wave of antimilitarism washed over Germany in the wake of the Kapp Putsch, penetrating deeply into Ebert's own Social Democratic party.

Lieut. Commander Hermann Ehrhardt *(right)* returns the salute of his brigade in March of 1920. Ehrhardt's crack unit, which was supposed to defend Berlin but decided to invade it, wore a distinctive insignia on its helmet *(above)*—a white swastika.

Charging Noske with laxity in controlling the generals, a number of leading Social Democrats overrode Ebert and forced the defense minister to resign. These Socialists also revived the call for the abolition of the faithless officers' corps and the creation of a democratic army to defend the republic. But before the movement could gain momentum, a fresh challenge burst upon the government.

The Communists and their allies were on the march once again in several areas of the Reich. The biggest uprising racked the Ruhr industrial district, where a so-called Red Army of 50,000 workers drove out the republic's forces. By March 20, three days after the collapse of the Kapp insurrection, rebels dominated the entire Ruhr east of Düsseldorf and Mühlheim. Ebert

Spectators run in panic as the Ehrhardt Brigade, withdrawing from Berlin after the failure of the Kapp Putsch, opens fire in response to a jeer from the crowd. A dozen bystanders died in the indiscriminate shooting.

could only turn to the officers who had so recently and conspicuously failed him. To fill the vacant post of commander of the Reichswehr, he promoted General Seeckt. The general, in turn, had little recourse but to call on the men who constituted the bulk of his command—the Freikorps, including the putschists of the Ehrhardt Brigade.

Descending on the Ruhr, the Freebooters extracted a furious revenge for the putsch's failure and the audacity of the workers in staging a strike. Over a two-week period, they obliterated the Red Army, killing or wounding a thousand Communists in the first two days alone.

With order restored, the Ebert government prudently decided not to press its case too hard against the leaders and participants in the Kapp Putsch. Kapp and General Lüttwitz were acquitted of all charges. The Freebooters of the Ehrhardt Brigade not only escaped the stockade but, incredibly, collected from the government the bonus of 16,000 gold marks the short-lived Kapp regime had promised them for overthrowing the republic. But their days in the Reichswehr were numbered nonetheless.

Seeckt was an officer of the old Prussian school, and he was determined to mold the 100,000 men allotted him by the Versailles treaty into a scrupulously selected and tightly disciplined army obedient to him, if to no one else. He dissolved the Ehrhardt Brigade and other Freikorps formations that, he wrote later, "were simply not suited for the work of peace."

Besides these military ramifications, the Kapp Putsch also left a political legacy. In the subsequent national elections held in June 1920, the three parties dedicated to preservation of the republic—the Social Democrats, the Centrists, and the Democrats—lost more than 40 percent of their previous vote. They wound up with less than half the seats in the Reichstag and, in fact, never again would achieve a majority. Many of those lost votes belonged to disgusted workers who switched to the far-left Independent Socialists. But the greatest gainers were the parties of the Right, which acquired a substantial segment of a middle class alienated by Versailles and the lawlessness still rampant in the land.

As confidence in the republic eroded and the strident cries of nationalists and racists grew louder, the Freebooters continued to make themselves felt. Subsidized by the radical right, many of the units had gone underground, had rearmed, and were training secretly under the cover of legitimate businesses that required large groups of strong young men—trucking companies, large farms, even traveling circuses. The most popular subterfuge was the labor camp, which allowed the Freebooters to indoctrinate a new generation of young men with the virus of racist nationalism, thus enabling them to serve as models for the Nazis a decade later.

Some of the more fanatical Freebooters took refuge in Bavaria and gath-

ered in secret societies dedicated to destroying the republic. Munich had been a haven for right-wing radicals ever since the spring of 1920, when ultranationalists, inspired by Kapp's example, ousted the legitimate state premier, a Socialist, and replaced him with an antirepublican conservative. A year later, Hermann Ehrhardt reassembled many members of his former brigade into what was called the Organization Consul. Under cover of the phony Wood Products Corporation, the Organization carried on its principal business: political terrorism. "Our struggle," said the Organization's journal, "is directed against the gravediggers of national thought, against democracy, social democracy, and Jewry."

The Organization Consul committed a substantial number of the 354 political murders that occurred in the three years after the official demise of the Freikorps. Among the first victims was Matthias Erzberger, the Center party leader who had signed the 1918 armistice and led the legislative fight to ratify the Versailles treaty. Ehrhardt's assassins pumped a dozen bullets into him as he strolled in the Black Forest one afternoon in August 1921. In June 1922, Philipp Scheidemann, the Social Democrat who had first proclaimed the republic, narrowly escaped blinding by Ehrhardt agents who squirted prussic acid into his eyes.

Three weeks later, a pair of thugs from the Organization committed one of the most senseless of the political killings. They lobbed a hand grenade and poured pistol fire into the auto of the foreign minister, Walther Rathenau, because he was Jewish and favored fulfillment of the Versailles reparations. The wealthy Rathenau, ironically, had raised more than $5 million to support the Freikorps.

Amid the turmoil and terrorism, one further element poisoned the political fortunes of the republic—runaway inflation. The decline in the value of the mark dated from the imperial government's decision to finance the war largely through debt instead of taxation. After the war, the interest on that debt and the high cost of demobilization and economic recovery contributed to chronic budget deficits. The republic, under pressure from business to hold down taxes, covered these shortfalls by printing more currency, driving the mark steadily downward.

The deficits—and the torrents of paper currency pouring off the presses—grew larger still after the Allies finally presented their bill for war reparations in April 1921. The demand was for annual payments, over several decades, of 132 billion marks in cash or in kind. Reeling under its impossible burdens, the mark by July 1922 had shrunk to less than one percent of its prewar value. Worth 4.2 marks to the dollar in 1914, the currency was now quoted at 493 marks to the dollar.

A cartoon *(inset)* depicts Clemenceau waiting to pounce on the Ruhr as French troops march into Essen.

A Unifying Humiliation in the Ruhr

France was looking for an excuse to invade the Ruhr, and when some telephone poles that were required as reparations were not delivered on time, the French army marched into Germany's 2,000-square-mile industrial heartland.

French brutality during the two-year occupation that followed united all Germans in hatred for their once and future enemy, and for that reason German nationalists considered it a godsend. Meanwhile, the German response—to shut down and sabotage all production in the Ruhr—delivered an additional blow to the staggering German economy.

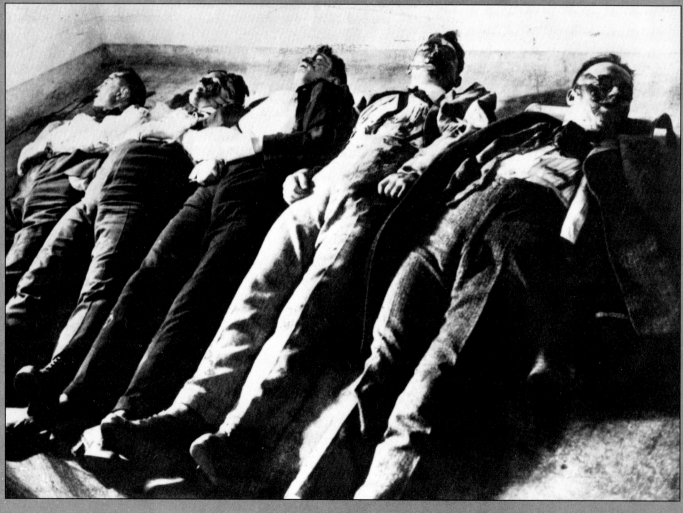

French guards menace a civilian in front of the main post office in Essen, principal city of the Ruhr, during the military occupation.

At left, the bodies of civilians shot for violating curfew are displayed in Essen as a warning to other Germans.

A French soldier stands guard over a railroad car of charcoal briquettes, a product of the Ruhr desperately needed in France.

But that was a mere prelude to the catastrophic plunge of 1923. The trigger was France's determination to occupy the Ruhr and thus glean every last pfennig of reparations. As a legal pretext, it announced that Germany had defaulted on its obligations by failing to deliver 140,000 telephone poles on the due date. In January 1923, the French and their Belgian allies marched into the Ruhr and seized its mines and industries.

The German government responded by cutting off all reparations payments to the French and launching a campaign of passive resistance against the occupiers. Throughout the Ruhr, commerce and industry came to a halt as workers walked off their jobs, officials refused to acknowledge the new French bosses, and saboteurs hit the transport system. To defend German borders against further incursions, the government even gave the

Officers of Berlin's Reichsbank carry baskets of currency that by late 1923 was almost worthless. To reduce the unwieldy volume of devalued banknotes required to buy anything, government printers turned out such astronomical denominations as the 10-billion-mark bill at right.

Freikorps its blessing once again. Thousands of Freebooters were called up to serve in the so-called Black Reichswehr, a secret reserve of 50,000 men that was patently illegal under the Versailles treaty.

The policy of passive resistance succeeded in thwarting the French, but at terrible cost. The German treasury was robbed of desperately needed revenue, and the lack of goods and raw materials disrupted the entire national economy. The decision to subsidize all those striking Ruhr workers caused new financial hemorrhages.

The descent of the mark gathered speed. When the French first occupied the Ruhr in January, the mark was worth 18,000 to the dollar. By July, it was down to 353,000 to the dollar and plummeting crazily out of control. By mid-November, the mark, in actual truth, was worth less than the paper it was printed on: One United States dollar equaled an incomprehensible 4.2 trillion marks. No fewer than 1,783 presses were running day and night to print ton after ton of this absurd currency.

A surrealistic inflation turned everyday life into a nightmare. Ordinary vegetables such as the humble kohlrabi cost 50 million marks each; a penny postage stamp cost as much as a fine Berlin home had in 1890. Housewives pushed wheelbarrows heaped high with currency through the streets just to purchase a pound of potatoes or a loaf of bread; a bit of margarine cost an entire day's wages. Businesses paid their employees daily, even twice a day, so they could hurry to buy food before prices doubled again. Many middle-class Germans, especially those on fixed incomes, fared even worse than the workers. Inflation wiped out their life savings and rendered investments like government bonds and insurance annuities worthless.

While suicide and mortality rates from other causes rose alarmingly among the working and middle classes, the profiteers got rich. Big land owners and industrialists liquidated their debts with depreciated marks and then acquired vast new holdings with bank and government loans that they paid off with worthless money.

The most astonishing of the profiteers was Hugo Stinnes, a conservative fifty-three-year-old member of the Reichstag who had already amassed a fortune in

heavy industry. By gobbling up inflation-stricken businesses with debt that was soon written off for practically nothing, Stinnes built an enormous empire that embraced literally hundreds of steel mills, chemical works, construction companies, banks, and oil refineries, plus no fewer than 150 newspapers and periodicals that reflected his right-wing views. Thousands of lesser predators took Stinnes as their beau ideal. "Never," wrote the novelist Stefan Zweig, had history "produced such madness in such gigantic proportions. All values were changed, and not only material ones; the laws of the state were flouted, no tradition, no moral code was respected, Berlin was transformed into the Babylon of the world. Bars, amusement parks, honky-tonks sprang up like mushrooms." In a sort of frantic denial of their plight, Germans of all ages and classes became inexhaustible dancers, prancing day and night to American jazz in hotels and ballrooms and nightclubs, on the street and at the beach. And they whistled a great deal, too—as if to keep up their courage.

In the autumn of 1923, the government finally acted decisively to halt the mounting economic calamity and civil ferment. A new cabinet had recently come to power under Gustav Stresemann, a monarchist and strong-willed leader of the conservative People's party, who was determined nonetheless to save the republic. Stresemann imposed a state of emergency to halt the strikes and insurrections, resumed reparations payments, ended passive resistance in the Ruhr, and took steps to stabilize the currency. These latter moves included balancing the budget and issuing a new temporary currency, the *Rentenmark*—equal in value to the prewar mark and backed by mortgage bonds based on the assets of the nation's entire industrial and agricultural establishment. He also forced speculators to sell the government $1.5 billion in foreign currency that they had accumulated, thereby doubling the Reichsbank's gold and foreign reserves. Stresemann's program proved successful: Inflation was stemmed, Germany went back to work, and the stage was set for economic rebirth.

Although the nightmare had ended, its trauma would haunt Germans for years to come, alienating them from democracy and accelerating the trend toward political extremism. Many workers would forsake their trade unions, which had been helpless in the face of inflation, and turn to the Communist movement. Newly impoverished members of the middle class, stunned by the perversion of lifelong values of thrift and frugality, would seek relief in the other direction. Blaming the inflation on the Weimar Republic, the Treaty of Versailles, and Jewish speculators, the embittered bourgeoisie would look for a strong authoritarian leader.

Meanwhile, in Bavaria, Germany's agony had turned up a strange and charismatic Austrian who meant to be the country's Führer. ✠

Victims of Germany's economic nightmare, a homeless, one-legged war veteran and his malnourished family are photographed in a Berlin shelter.

Civilians in business suits man a machine-gun post in a Berlin street. The city's radicals were called to arms in 1919 by *The Red Flag (inset)*, official publication of the Spartacus League.

Berlin's Red Revolt

"We are fighting for the gates of heaven," proclaimed the Communist leader Karl Liebknecht, rallying his Spartacus League to seize Berlin and take over the German government during the first days of 1919. Indeed, for German Communists and thousands of leftist sympathizers, never were the stakes higher, nor the portals of victory nearer, than during that fateful time. Germany seemed ripe for Communist plucking. The new republic's beleaguered chancellor, Friedrich Ebert, had failed to quash the radical challenge with the diminished resources at hand—military units in chaos and divided in their loyalties, and a Berlin police force that seemed indifferent to the threat.

Early in January, the Spartacists and their supporters seized control of Berlin's utilities, transportation system, and munitions factories. When the Ebert government fired the city's police chief, a Spartacist sympathizer, Liebknecht and his Communist coleader, Rosa Luxemburg, called a mass demonstration on January 5 to protest the dismissal.

On that day and the ones that followed, hundreds of thousands of workers poured into the streets, brandishing weapons, waving red flags, and shouting revolutionary slogans. In a last-ditch effort to restore order and save the government, Ebert and his defense minister, Gustav Noske, summoned help from the only remaining source: the Freikorps, or Free Corps, paramilitary bands of right-wing volunteers who had been training and drilling in camps in the countryside. The Freikorps units responded eagerly to the government's plea, setting out for Berlin at quick march, and the stage was set for bloody confrontation.

Rifles at the shoulder, Spartacist
supporters march to occupy
Berlin's chief newspaper-
publishing district.

Rebels without a Plan

On January 5, Spartacist leaders joined the deposed police chief in Berlin's main police station to plot strategy. Chancellor Ebert and other government leaders took refuge in the chancellery, which was soon surrounded by an angry leftist mob. Elsewhere, armed rebels roamed free, taking over the Belle-Alliance Platz, Berlin's publishing district, and occupying the offices of some of the city's newspapers, including that of *Vorwärts*, the organ of the rival Socialists. That evening, the leaders of the rebellion voted to fight the government until it was overthrown. No one, however, devised a plan for accomplishing this. On January 6, the protesters captured the government's printing plant, its news agency, and Berlin's main telegraph office. For days, the crowd waited restlessly as the men who were besieged in police headquarters deliberated.

At the Mosse publishing house, former soldiers join civilian rebels behind a barricade of newsprint rolls and bundled newspapers.

Organizing a Rescue

While the Spartacists vacillated, Defense Minister Gustav Noske retreated to the western suburb of Dahlem to engineer the retaking of Berlin. Guarded by Freikorps units from nearby Zossen and equipped with a single telephone, Noske made contact with former army officers in and around the capital. Within days, they had recruited thousands of Freikorps troops to rescue Ebert's government.

On January 10, 350 Freikorps soldiers based near the northern suburb of Spandau overpowered Spartacists attempting to take control of the huge munitions plant there. By the next morning, 1,200 Freikorps troops from Potsdam had attacked the Belle-Alliance Platz, blasting the *Vorwärts* building with howitzers and trench mortars at point-blank range. The Spartacists inside fired back, but their machine guns and rifles were no match for artillery, and soon the rebels were overrun.

Dead and wounded Berliners lie sprawled on the cobblestones as Spartacists and helmeted Freikorps troops fight hand to hand on a residential street.

Deployed at the feet of the great bronze horses atop the Brandenburg Gate, government loyalists cover a broad field of fire with their machine gun.

The Loyalists Resurgent

On January 11, Defense Minister Noske led more than 3,000 Freikorps troops to the heart of Berlin. As they passed through the city's prosperous western suburbs, residents lined the streets and cheered. "Many a patriotic heart could once again rejoice at a sorely missed sight," declared a conservative newspaper. "Soldiers were marching across the Potsdamer Platz, soldiers with officers, soldiers controlled by their leaders."

Unchallenged, Noske's men marched to the Brandenburg Gate, where they relieved government loyalists who had wrested the symbolic landmark from the Spartacists a few hours earlier. Then, the defense minister's military advisers divided the city into sectors and the Freikorps fanned out, setting up their machine guns at important intersections and laying siege to public buildings that were still in Communist hands.

Inside commandeered barracks at Berlin University, Freikorps troops prepare their equipment for the street-fighting to come.

Civilians scatter before Berlin's club-wielding police. Some policemen, daunted by the overwhelming odds, took up the fight only after the Freikorps arrived.

Massacre from the Right

Giving vent to a virulent hatred of communism, Freikorps troops descended on the radicals with rare savagery. At Spandau, Spartacists who were not killed in action were captured and then murdered on the way to jail. At the *Vorwärts* building, six men who emerged under white flags of truce were nevertheless shot on the spot.

The killing continued. After pounding police headquarters with artillery, a company of Noske's men stormed the building and slaughtered Spartacists in offices, hallways, and elevators. While some of the radicals were shot where they stood, others met an even worse fate: They were kicked and chased from room to room before being clubbed to death with rifle butts.

Stretcher-bearers risk gunfire to evacuate a casualty of the clash between Freikorps troops and Spartacists on January 12.

An Uneasy End to Bloodshed

By January 15, the Freikorps had imposed an uneasy calm upon the capital. Machine guns and armored cars cowed most dissenters, and sharpshooters picked off the occasional Spartacist sniper.

The Spartacist leaders, Liebknecht and Luxemburg, had gone into hiding, but Freikorps men tracked them down. The two radicals were taken to Freikorps headquarters in Berlin's Eden Hotel. Late that night, they were escorted separately through a rear door, clubbed to the ground, spirited away in automobiles, and shot along the road.

They were the last to be murdered in Berlin's week of bloodshed. More than a hundred Spartacists died for their cause, but the Freikorps emerged from the violence with only thirteen dead and twenty wounded.

In the months that followed, Ebert used the Freikorps to quell dissent throughout Germany. Eventually, however, these erstwhile soldiers would turn on the republic that gave them sanction and help sow the seeds of nazism.

After meeting with Freikorps officers under a flag of truce, Spartacist leaders in the newspaper district return to their men to discuss surrender.

A Party Built on Hate

Penniless and rootless, burning with rage and humiliation, Adolf Hitler, like many of his comrades, looked to the army for shelter and succor. The Reichswehr had been his home, the agent of his self-respect, the only meaning in his life for the past four years; it was to him the repository of every Germánic virtue. And so, after his discharge from the hospital in Pasewalk, Hitler hurried to rejoin the List Regiment's reserve battalion in Munich in late November 1918. But what had become of his beloved unit he found dismaying, and it fed his fury at Germany's downfall. All discipline seemed to have vanished. In its place ruled a sort of mad egalitarianism and loathsome bolshevism.

Control of the barracks had fallen to haphazard leftist gatherings known as soldiers' councils, whose conclusions were subject to something called voluntary obedience—which in practice meant disobedience. Worse, enlisted men roamed the streets, accosting and insulting officers, ripping off their decorations, epaulets, and cap cockades. To Corporal Hitler, proud holder of the Iron Cross, First Class, the situation was intolerable. He volunteered for duty at Traunstein, an isolated camp sixty miles from Munich, where for the next few months he guarded some remaining Russian prisoners of war.

On his lonely rounds, the twenty-nine-year-old Austrian expatriate had ample time to contemplate Germany's betrayal by the so-called November Criminals in Berlin, the vengeful demands of the Allies, the rampaging Bolsheviks, and, above all, the Jews, who he was sure were to blame for it all. "At this time," he wrote later, "plans chased themselves through my head, one after another. For days I pondered what could be done, if anything at all. But at the end of every deliberation came the sobering thought that I, in my utter obscurity, had not even the slightest basis for any practical action."

That would come soon enough. Throughout Germany events were conspiring to speed Adolf Hitler toward his destiny. The Bavaria to which he had returned was in a turmoil that matched his own. No city had reacted more violently to the collapse of the Second Reich than excitable, flam-

Rallying in Munich in January 1923, members of the nascent Nazi party display an assortment of crude swastikas, symbol of the Aryan nation Adolf Hitler intended to create.

boyant Munich with its many breweries and its hearty, emotional people. A few days before the November 9 Berlin revolution, the Bavarian monarchy—the last of the Wittelsbach dynasty—was overthrown, and a free-thinking Jewish journalist, Kurt Eisner, was installed as minister-president. Eisner's dreamy and ineffectual administration ("a Punch-and-Judy show in real life," hooted a Berlin newspaper) lasted scarcely a hundred days before he was assassinated on February 21 by a reactionary young nobleman and army officer. A leftist coalition of workers, soldiers, and peasants assumed power, called for a general strike, and declared a state of siege. Trucks with mounted machine guns manned by Marxists rolled through the streets, bullhorns blaring "Revenge for Eisner." Communists occupied the banks, hotels, and other public buildings; an iron censorship was clapped on the press; and large numbers of prominent citizens were rounded up and imprisoned as hostages.

When word reached Munich that a Communist regime under the fanatical Bela Kun had taken power in Hungary, the news galvanized Munich's Marxists to oust Eisner's successor, Johannes Hoffmann. With a roar of revolution, leftist leaders declared a Soviet government in place. But Communist rule was to be brief—for a "White Terror" was in the making. Down from the north came units of the Reichswehr and the Freikorps, most notably the Ehrhardt Brigade with swastika-emblazoned helmets and a taste for killing. At Puchheim, the troops slaughtered fifty-two Russian POWs who had been released by the German Reds; a column of medics en

Corporal Hitler (*fifth from the left*) is photographed with his unit shortly after the war. Instead of being mustered out, Hitler volunteered for duty guarding prisoners of war who were waiting to be repatriated.

route to treat Marxist wounded met the same fate. At Perlach, a dozen noncombatant workers were shot, and captured German Communists were executed out of hand.

On the final day of the Red regime, a panicky official made the terrible error of ordering the death of rightist hostages the Communists were holding. Ten prisoners were slain, including a prince, a painter, a sculptor, a railroad official, a baron, and a young countess—all people that the average German was inclined to admire. That the executions took place in a schoolyard only heightened the revulsion as news of the deed swept through Munich. The next day—May 1—Reichswehr and Freikorps troops broke into the city from all sides, and with mortars and hand grenades cleaned out the Red strongholds. Corpses littered the streets. The troops went from house to house exacting retribution for the hostages by hauling out suspected Marxists for a drumhead trial and execution. Munich's dalliance with the Left was ended forever.

Hitler took no part in these events. He had returned in March from Traunstein to his regiment's barracks, and there he remained. In later years, he told of facing down with his carbine three Reds who came one day to arrest him. But there is no evidence to bolster his word. In any event, with the triumph of the Right, his destiny was beckoning. In the army purge that followed, Hitler testified with merciless exactness against fellow soldiers who had gone over to the revolution. Many of them faced firing squads as a consequence. But to Hitler it was not a matter of turning informant. He detested and feared the Left. Red armbands had made these men not comrades but enemies. His performance caught the eye of a Captain Karl Mayr, who made him an undercover agent and sent him to an anti-Communist indoctrination course sponsored by the army at the University of Munich. There, Hitler added to the core of superficial knowledge that fed his hate-laden theories of conspiracy. One day, listening with growing anger to someone defending Jews, he stepped forward to answer the man. In his fervent denunciation—and in subsequent lectures to members of his regiment—he found his great weapon, a faculty that would have a cataclysmic effect on the future of humankind: "I knew how to speak!"

Others would shortly perceive that fantastic gift: A professor recalled soldiers "standing spellbound around a man who was vehemently haranguing them in a strangely guttural voice, and with mounting passion. I had the peculiar feeling that the man was feeding on the excitement which he himself had whipped up. I saw a pale, thin face and hair hanging down the forehead over a close-cropped mustache; his strikingly large, pale blue eyes shone with a cold fanatical light."

Mayr monitored the right-wing political clubs that abounded in Munich and had an illicit army fund to assist any that looked promising. On September 12, 1919, he instructed Hitler to don civilian clothes and look in on a scruffy handful who called themselves the German Workers' party (*Deutsche Arbeiterpartei*, or DAP). The meeting was in a back room of a beer cellar known as the Sterneckerbräu. In this society of many breweries, superb beer, and dedicated drinkers, beer cellars were the homes of many such groups. While plump waitresses circulated with a never-ending supply of foaming mugs, drinkers at tables listened to speeches, ready to pound their mugs in thunderous approval or send them flying like missiles. The atmosphere was rowdy, fatal to a weak speaker but perfect for an Adolf Hitler. At the Sterneckerbräu that evening, the audience of about four dozen was snoring over a series of boring speeches, and Hitler was on the point of leaving, when a certain Professor Baumann took the floor to advocate Bavarian secession from Germany and *Anschluss*, or union, with Austria.

This was a common view in Bavaria, where the genial, volatile people felt out of tune with the stiff-necked Prussians to the north. But it was anathema to Hitler. His dream of somehow connecting himself to German greatness depended on the existence of a powerfully united nation. He rose and in fifteen fiery minutes so devastated the professor that the poor man "left the hall like a wet poodle," as Hitler later put it. Afterward, the party's chairman, Anton Drexler, pressed a pamphlet on Hitler and urged him to return. In the pink-covered, forty-page booklet, Hitler found echoes of his own half-baked theories of hate and conspiracy.

Drexler, thirty-five, a quiet, square-set man, was a machinist, a true worker but one who had no use for unions or the Left. He connected, in fact, to the ultranationalist, archly right-wing Thule Society, with 1,500 influential members scattered about Bavaria. The society used the swastika as its symbol and published a newspaper, the *Münchener Beobachter;* the paper was racist to the core, dwelling on the glories of Aryan blood and the horrors of its dilution by that of inferior Jews and Slavs. The society had contacted Drexler because it hoped to foment a workers' revolution but knew nothing about workers. One of its members, Karl Harrer, a sportswriter, teamed with Drexler to form what they called the Political Workers' Circle, which shortly became the DAP. At first, Hitler spurned this inconsequential band, whose office and treasury were a cigar box containing a few papers and exactly seven marks. "Dreadful, dreadful," he snorted. But then he began to see the potential. "This absurd little group with its handful of members seemed to me to have the advantage that it was not petrified into an 'organization,'" he later wrote. It could be an ideal tool, offering him, for the first time in his life, a chance to lead, to be a Führer.

Munich's Brush with Anarchy

Stirred by local Communist leaders, thousands of workers rampaged through Munich on February 21, 1919, following the assassination of Minister-President Kurt Eisner *(right)*. After two months of near anarchy, the central government moved to reestablish its authority by dispatching 30,000 Freikorps troops to the troubled city.

On May 1, these hard-boiled fighters burst into Munich with guns blazing and—with the help of other rightists—slaughtered 1,000 suspected Communists. Order was restored, but Munich was left a city rife with scores to be settled.

Kurt Eisner, Bavaria's minister-president, rides to a meeting during his brief regime.

Flaunting the red flag of communism, soldiers and workers throng downtown Munich after the murder of Eisner in 1919.

PANZERAUTO WELCHES ERFOLGREICH
IN DIE KÄMPFE EINGRIFF
MÜNCHEN 2 MAI. 19
Phot. H. HOFFMANN
Schellingstr. 50.

From his rooftop vantage point,
a sniper keeps watch on a street
in the Bavarian capital. The
Freikorps lost only seventy men
in the brief, bloody campaign.

In an armored car embellished with a death's-head, Freikorps soldiers roll into Munich. One officer told his men, "It is a lot better to kill a few innocent people than to let one guilty person escape."

Dressed in Bavarian folk costume, men of the Volunteer Citizens' Defense forces march through Munich. After seizing the city, the coalition of rightists pulled red Communist flags from windows and ran up the white-and-blue of Bavaria.

Wearing a fedora, Hitler stands second from the left in a photograph of an early membership drive for the German Workers' party. The card above shows that Hitler joined the party in January 1920. At his behest, the group changed its name to the National Socialist German Workers' party, a cumbersome title that was shortened to Nazi.

With Captain Mayr's blessing, Hitler devoted himself fully to the DAP. Heretofore, the dismally attended meetings had been announced by notes passed from hand to hand or posted on bulletin boards. But Hitler scraped together enough money for an advertisement in the *Münchener Beobachter* and on October 16 held the party's first genuine public meeting in the cellar of the Hofbräuhaus. Hitler fretted that no one would come, but 111 people turned up, almost filling the room. Hitler shortly had them howling approval and beating their mugs on the tables with his diatribe on Germany's betrayal by the conspirators and Jews in Berlin. When the hat was passed afterward, the take was a stunning 300 marks. Hitler pressed for a larger meeting at which they would charge half a mark admission. Other political parties never charged, yet on November 13, even more people paid their half a mark to hear Hitler excoriate the Versailles treaty and scream: "We must stand up and fight for the idea that things cannot go on this way. German misery must be broken by German iron."

The party now had its own office, Captain Mayr paying the rent, and Hitler hired a business manager. The meetings grew larger. Hitler ordered posters of blood red, knowing that the Communist color would enrage the leftists and draw hecklers—who could in turn be violently silenced. It would make for an exciting evening—politics as theater. The police began monitoring the meetings but did nothing to interfere. Hitler, still a barracks soldier, formed a cadre of tough veterans into *Ordnertruppen*, or monitor

In 1920, the party rented a beer hall's back room for its headquarters. "It was a small vaulted room," Hitler wrote. "On overcast days, everything was dark. We brightened the walls with posters announcing our meetings and for the first time hung up our new flag."

troops, to deal with the hecklers. These bully boys would grow into the party's Storm Troopers—"swift as greyhounds, tough as leather, hard as Krupp steel," was how Hitler characterized them.

On February 24, 1920, the DAP staged its biggest meeting to date. More than 2,000 people packed into the Hofbräuhaus, while the Ordnertruppen stood ready to smash dissenters' heads. Hitler electrified his audience. On this night he read the famous Twenty-Five Points he and Drexler had drafted that would become the basis of nazism. The manifesto laid out four major themes—revenge for Versailles by territorial expansion; vaguely Marxist views against capitalism that in later years Hitler would not let interfere with his courtship of German industrialists; sanctions against Jews; and a recipe for government that sounded platitudinous but was actually the groundwork for a dictatorship. The heart of the latter was

read in thundering tones: Common good before individual good.

When Hitler finished speaking, men leaped onto chairs and tables, and the huge beer hall reverberated with what a reporter termed a "monstrous uproar." As he watched the Hofbräuhaus empty that night, Hitler sensed that an event of great significance for him had taken place, and he later put his feelings in writing. In one version, he pictured the meeting as kindling the fires to forge a new sword of Siegfried for the liberation of Germany. In another, he wrote: "When I finally closed the meeting, I was not alone in thinking that a wolf had been born that was destined to break into the herd of deceivers and misleaders of the people."

Throughout the year 1920, the party collected members until by December, 3,000 dedicated members were on the rolls, and many thousands more were sympathizers. The DAP renamed itself the National Socialist German Workers' party, NSDAP. The first two syllables in German broke down to an easy nickname: Nazis. Hitler chose its symbol, the swastika. Out of the army now and living in a single shabby room, he devoted days to finding the most forceful possible design for this symbol, finally settling on broad black strokes on a white background against a field of provocative red.

The party was Hitler's life. He had virtually no friends, either male or female, for it was his peculiarity that while he could commune with an audience of thousands, he could not reach out to individuals. But he was a natural orator, not only in tune with his listeners' anguish and hunger but capable of a transcendental rapport with them, until the roaring voice shrieking out amid the heavy fumes of beer and cigar smoke in murky halls became the very expression of themselves.

He began as their own minds worked, hesitantly, and then, feeling their emotion, his sentences began to soar, his breath quickened, his eyes glittered with passion, and soon the words crashed against the audience in waves, at once exalting it and making it captive. "In this unlikely-looking creature there dwelt a miracle: his voice, a guttural thunder," said an observer, Konrad Heiden. Another contemporary, Otto Strasser, said, "He touches each private wound in the raw, liberating the mass unconscious, expressing its innermost aspirations, telling it what it most wants to hear." After exploring the pain of postwar Germany, blaming all its troubles on the Jews, promising a future full of glory with oppressors destroyed, Hitler liked to end with his arm flung out, screeching, "Deutschland! Deutschland! Deutschland!" The words rang hoarsely in deathly silence—and then came the frenzied applause, mugs pounding like a cannonade.

After a speech of two or three hours, Hitler would be sweating in his tight blue suit and high collar, satiation and calm in his expression as the

A worshipful artist elevated
Hitler to Messianic stature in
this widely distributed painting
and borrowed its title from the
Bible: *Am Anfang das Wort* (In
the beginning was the Word).
A contemporary noted that
Hitler "could play like a virtuoso
on the well-tempered piano of
middle-class hearts."

outpouring of love—albeit based on hate—washed over him. Men around him felt that nothing so gratified him as feeling the power of an audience prostrate at his feet. And certainly nothing else so strengthened the party.

Such a talent is beyond explanation, and Hitler worked hard to refine and improve his image and technique. He affected a trench coat and black velour hat and carried a heavy dog whip as a scepter of authority. He practiced gestures, watched comics control audiences, took acting lessons, evaluated acoustics, and thought deeply on shaping his message. He used only a few ideas and drove them again and again into peoples' minds. If you lie, he said, lie big, for a little of even the most outrageous lie will stick if you press it hard enough. Never hesitate, never qualify, never concede a shred of validity or even decency to the other side. Attack, attack, attack!

By July of 1921, Hitler was in a position to demand full control of the party. On threat of resignation, he forced Drexler and the others to grant him supremacy. From then on, when Hitler signed a document, he appended under his name "der Führer der NSDAP" (Leader of the NSDAP). At first, he focused on securing his rule and preparing the party to spread beyond Bavaria to all of Germany. He streamlined the office with a new business manager, Max Amann, to handle membership and the increasingly substantial finances. He set up a three-man action committee with himself as head and, below that, six working committees led by his loyalists.

Hermann Esser, a former journalist and a fluent speaker, became propaganda chief. Dietrich Eckart took over as editor of the *Völkischer Beobachter*, the renamed *Münchener Beobachter*, which the party had purchased from the Thule Society with money supplied partly by Mayr's secret army account. Both extolled Hitler and the concept of *Führerprinzip*, or rule with an iron hand. A poet, journalist, and translator of some note, Eckart had a rough proletarian appearance but was nonetheless welcome in society salons as well as in beer halls. He was Hitler's elder by twenty years and made himself, if not quite a father figure, at least as much a confidant as Hitler's nature allowed. Clever and literate, he fed Hitler's jumbled sense of Wagnerian myth and Nordic glory that so captivated audiences. He also introduced the young agitator into circles of wealth and position, polishing Hitler's manners as they went. Before long, powerful people began tumbling into the trap that had ensnared Drexler—they imagined they could use Hitler, when in fact the opposite was true.

One of Eckart's protégés was a refugee Estonian, Alfred Rosenberg, who introduced the Führer to the infamous *Protocols of the Elders of Zion;* this scurrilous forgery purporting to be the text of a Jewish plot for world domination had long since been discredited. Nevertheless, it fitted Hitler's

need for a conspiracy of Jews, so he believed it the rest of his life and used it with terrible effect. Rosenberg became a principal party thinker and the architect of its dogma: the superiority of the Teutonic master race and its inherent right to rule; the sacred beauty of violence and war; the biological and spiritual inferiority of Jews.

There were others who would loom large in Nazi history: Rudolf Hess, who had been an officer in Hitler's wartime regiment, would come to serve his Führer with doglike devotion; Captain Ernst Röhm, an army officer still on active duty, would funnel arms to the party; Hermann Göring, a dashing aviator and wartime hero with Germany's highest award for valor, the Pour le mérite (the Blue Max), would eventually become Hitler's second-in-command. Röhm and Göring in particular would play crucial roles in the Storm Troopers, the gangs of bloody-minded youths emerging as the strong-arm element of the party.

Violence had always been central to Hitler's views. It drew attention, instilled fear, commanded respect, led to domination. In August of 1921, Hitler reorganized the Ordnertruppen and gave them the cover name *Sportabteilung*, or Sports Section, but within a month decided to call the organization what it was, the *Sturmabteilung* (SA), or Storm Section. By whatever name, the SA's role went far beyond mere protection of Nazi rallies. Largely recruited from army veterans and organized into paramilitary squads of 100 men, the SA drilled on country roads and fields, then went into Munich's streets looking for trouble.

Gangs of Storm Troopers armed with truncheons swarmed over leftist gatherings, pummeling faces and cracking heads. Hitler declared that his SA men would "ruthlessly prevent all meetings or lectures likely to distract the minds of our fellow countrymen." Jews evoked a special ferocity: Synagogues were desecrated, and Jews were beaten in the streets. Storm Troopers circulated through beer halls with boxes inscribed "Contribute for the Jew massacre." But leftists and Jews were only two of the targets. Anyone or anything that provoked Nazi displeasure was at risk; the SA even invaded theaters to shout down performances of plays the Führer considered decadent. Hitler understood that power lay in control of public places: It was a Nazi axiom that "whoever conquers the streets conquers the masses, and whoever conquers the masses conquers the state."

Hitler became a master propagandist. Everything was calculated for effect. At the start he chose red as his color for its high impact. He adopted the swastika for its association with the *völkisch* movement and because the Ehrhardt Brigade had made it stand for assertion of the Teutonic will. He presented the symbol lavishly—on armbands, lapel pins, banners,

ever-larger flags. He loved ceremony, parades, fierce young men, marching music, singing, chanting, vast banks of color. He staged flag ceremonies, the standards dipping and wheeling as the band blared; color, symbol, sight, sound all assaulting the senses in a weird combination of theater and opera and high mass and the flavor of war. The crowds grew larger, and Hitler staged numbers of rallies at once, racing from one to another. His entrances were always dramatic: a speaker suddenly interrupted in midsentence by the great man's abrupt appearance at the door, the room resounding with shouts of "Heil!", Hitler striding forward to harangue the crowd.

The startling growth of the party in this period was a direct reflection of increasing turmoil in Bavaria. Hitler spoke openly for revolution. His aim, often stated, was to demolish the Berlin government, which he considered soft, decadent, Marxist. He wanted to hang the November Criminals from lampposts. Bavarians reveled in such talk. Recruits joined in such numbers that membership rolls fell weeks behind. The party probably had about 6,000 members at the start of 1922, and that August an outdoor Nazi rally drew 50,000 spectators, who watched 600 Storm Troopers parade past. By the end of 1922, police estimated 10,000 members. The following year, the Nazis enrolled 35,000 new members, and the SA grew to nearly 15,000.

Hitler was demonstrating to all Bavaria that he and his Nazis were a force to be reckoned with. That was the purpose of his visit to Coburg, a strongly Socialist town 140 miles north of Munich. In October 1922, rightists there invited Hitler to celebrate German Day and suggested that he might bring along "some gentlemen of your company." Seizing the opportunity, Hitler arrived on a special train with 800 men, a military band, and a blizzard of Nazi banners. It was tantamount to a declaration of war against Coburg's Socialists. Fearing trouble, the police forbade the Nazis to march out of the station in ranks, or with their forty-two-piece band playing and flags flying. Hitler ignored the command. "I ordered the flags and music to go in front, and the procession was formed," he later wrote.

First came eight huge Storm Troopers, then the standard-bearers, and then Hitler, striding at the head of his men. As the parade left the station, a crowd of Socialist workers started yelling "Murderers!" "Criminals!" "Bandits!" "Hoodlums!" Cobblestones and roofing tiles rained down on the Nazi ranks, and groups of men charged the marchers swinging iron rods and nail-studded clubs. Hitler turned and signaled with his walking stick— at which cue the Storm Troopers went to work. They were splendidly trained in street-fighting tactics, and in minutes the street was clear. The Socialists regrouped and tried again, and again were thrashed by the disciplined Nazis, this time with the aid of the police, "who shared our enthusiastic dislike for street rabble," as one Nazi recalled.

An Ancient Talisman Revived

By most accounts, the hooked cross that Adolf Hitler selected to symbolize his movement had its origins 6,000 years ago in the Middle East. Derived from a Sanskrit word meaning "object of well-being," the swastika has since appeared throughout Europe and Asia on items ranging from Greek vases to Hindu temples. Nineteenth-century German scholars claimed this good-luck symbol as an ancient Teutonic sign, and by 1912, half a dozen ultranationalist groups were using it on their stationery and periodicals. Commercial firms marketed swastika tie clips, belt buckles, and other gimcracks to meet a burgeoning demand for symbols of Germany's heritage.

When Hitler solicited designs for a Nazi flag in 1920, his followers inundated him with sketches, most of them incorporating the swastika. He modified a drawing that had been submitted by a Bavarian dentist and came up with the flag that would soon arouse fear and loathing in some, blind devotion in others. Although he initially rejected the colors red, black, and white, Hitler concluded that his design breathed life into the old imperial colors. "It was young and new, like the movement itself," he wrote. "It had the effect of a burning torch."

One of the earliest-known swastikas appears on the pottery bowl below, which was found in Samarra (ancient Baghdad) and dates to about 4000 BC.

Of his party's new banner Hitler wrote: "In red we see the social idea of the movement, in white the nationalist idea, in the swastika the mission of Aryan man's struggle for victory."

That evening, Hitler gave one of his best speeches before a thousand roaring rightists, offering the Nazi party as the solution to every problem and ending: "Our swastika is not the symbol of an organization, but rather a victory banner. It will and must fly above the palace in Berlin and the peasant's hut alike. Resurrection through readiness to act is our answer for the great German fatherland that is coming."

The Storm Troopers marched through Coburg again the next day, and the strength of the Nazis had a remarkable effect on the citizens: Old imperial German flags appeared in windows, and people cheered as the SA men marched past. After two days in Coburg, Hitler and his legion boarded their train and rumbled into the night. Throughout Germany, newspapers echoed the headline in the *Coburg Volksblatt:* "Coburg under the control of Hitler. Capitulation of the state to the Hitler guardsmen."

It should not have surprised Hitler that the Coburg police had come over to his side. By and large, police everywhere had a visceral dislike of the Left, and in Munich, the Nazis had long enjoyed the cooperation of the authorities. Dr. Wilhelm Frick, head of the political division of the Munich police, later explained, "We recognized that this movement should not be suppressed. We saw in the party the seeds of Germany's renewal. That is why we held our protecting hands over Herr Hitler." This attitude radiated from the top. The Munich police commissioner, Ernst Pöhner, warmly supported Hitler. The tall, aristocratic Pöhner achieved enduring fame for a single quip. Told that political murders were being committed in Bavaria, he peered through his pince-nez and said, "Yes, but not enough of them!" Pöhner blunted the growing complaints about Nazi storm tactics, and the most outrageous conduct never drew more than a nominal penalty. Once, Hitler served a month in jail after a particularly violent episode, during which he had joined in beating up a secessionist politician. But in general, Munich officials gave him free rein because they agreed with his aims and his tactics.

The real power, however, lay at the state level and with that portion of the German army stationed in Bavaria. Though supposedly subordinate to Berlin, Bavaria had a more or less autonomous government headed by a minister-president. After November of 1922, that office was held by Eugen von Knilling, who was widely recognized as a front for Gustav von Kahr, whom everyone expected to take over in any crisis.

Kahr was a squat, devious man who sat with his massive head thrust

Gustav von Kahr, dedicated to restoring the Bavarian monarchy, became state commissioner of Bavaria in September 1923. His role in suppressing the November Beer Hall Putsch marked him for death once the Nazis came to power.

forward from between hunched shoulders. Conservative to the core, he was an ardent monarchist who wanted nothing so much as a return of the Wittelsbachs to the Bavarian throne in the person of the current pretender, Crown Prince Rupprecht. Kahr had served briefly as minister-president after the Freikorps put down the Communist uprising in 1919 and had quarreled with Berlin immediately. He neither liked nor trusted Hitler, who responded in kind, but each man expected to use the other, and so they circled one another cautiously.

Both understood that no grab for power, no putsch, could succeed without the support, or at least the acquiescence, of the Bavarian state police and the army. As of the moment, neither of those organizations seemed anxious to see Hitler in control. The police were commanded by an ambitious young aristocrat, Colonel Hans Ritter von Seisser, whose position could scarcely have been more clear. Through the interior minister, Seisser warned that his men would shoot down putschists in the streets. Hitler gave his promise not to initiate a putsch, which was honest in its way. He did not wish to rule Bavaria; he meant to rule Germany with Bavaria's help. Throughout all that followed, he saw himself and the Bavarian authorities as basically on the same side.

The true key to the unfolding drama was the Reichswehr, under the command of an elegant and icy Prussian, General Hans von Seeckt. The army was the only national power center left in Germany, and it was intent both on survival and on the destruction of the Marxists. From the first, the army had been hiding weapons the Allies had ordered destroyed—not merely small arms and ammunition, but also artillery, trucks, and armored cars. On occasion, weapons were checked out to select rightist organizations for use against the Left. And in Bavaria, the man in charge of this distribution was Ernst Röhm, an ardent Nazi.

Captain Röhm was a hearty Bavarian soldier, short, powerful, and ruddy. He had been mutilated in war when the bridge of his nose was shot away. He served as political adviser to the commander of the Bavarian section of the army and had followed Mayr as godfather to Munich's rightist groups. Röhm had joined Hitler's party at the start and was critical to its success. As Eckart gave Hitler social acceptance, so Röhm gave him standing in military circles and recruited the troops who formed the nucleus of the SA. Röhm's outlook was simple: "I am a soldier. Europe—the whole world—can go up in flames. What is that to us? Germany must live and be free."

As it happened, Röhm got a new commanding general early in 1923. The independent-minded Bavarians were a constant trial to the national government in Berlin, and this applied equally to the army. Although Bavarian troops were sworn to uphold the nation, their deeper loyalty often seemed

to be to their state. Thus, in those chaotic times, with all the talk of putsch, Seeckt felt it prudent to send a fresh leader, General Otto von Lossow, to make sure that the units in Bavaria understood who gave the orders.

Röhm presented Hitler to Lossow. The new general was an aristocrat, and he could barely conceal his contempt for the putative dictator, whom he considered an ignorant though effective rabble-rouser. Lossow's own position was ambiguous. A Bavarian himself, he shared his province's frustrations and was close to the strongman Kahr, with his monarchist notions. But this was a time when no one knew what would happen next, and men with power, political or military, were wondering which way to jump. Lossow would be a major factor in the drama to come; he wondered if Hitler might be useful and decided to give him some rope.

There was a military wild card on the scene as well. The renowned General Erich Ludendorff, out of the army but still a commanding presence to active soldiers and veterans alike, had fled to Munich from Berlin after the failure of the Kapp Putsch in 1920. Feeling secure in this city of rightists, he entertained a stream of visitors. Scarcely a plot unfolded to which he was not privy; he listened to all, yet committed himself to none. Hitler had been courting him for more than a year when Lossow arrived. The former corporal and the former general got on as might have been expected, Hitler obsequious and Ludendorff contemptuous.

By the beginning of 1923, Germany's problems were catastrophic. The accelerating collapse of the mark and the French presence in the Ruhr had Bavarian nationalists in an uproar. Hitler readily incorporated these events into his litany of hate, crying that the whole problem was the rotting democracy in Berlin dominated, in his demonic belief, by a vast conspiracy of Jews. This raw-meat diet fed the party's growth but raised expectations ever higher. The SA restlessly awaited its marching orders. The men expected a putsch any day.

A sign of Hitler's mounting strength came in January, when he ordered a massive Party Day, featuring a gathering of the faithful at a dozen rallies and a marching formation of thousands of SA men. Reviewing these plans against insistent rumors of a Nazi putsch, Bavarian authorities decided to ban the entire affair. Hitler was stunned, since he felt that he was doing the Bavarian state's work for it. He immediately understood that to back down would destroy his image among his followers. He had no choice but to hurl the gauntlet. The Nazis would march anyway. Let the police fire. Hitler would take the first bullet himself. "Two hours after the first shot, the regime will be finished!" he roared. Then, somewhat more humbly, he appealed to General Lossow, who reluctantly interceded with the author-

Flouting a ban on public meetings, 20,000 Nazis poured into Munich for Party Day, which was actually three days of rallies that began on January 27, 1923. The following day, 2,000 of the faithful gathered at Munich's Marsfeld for the presentation of swastika-emblazoned standards to newly formed Storm Trooper units.

ities. Hitler would be permitted to hold six of his twelve beer-hall rallies but was forbidden to parade his SA outdoors. The Führer agreed—and then held all twelve and his massed outdoor formation as well. The message was clear: In Munich, the Nazis rivaled the government.

In May, however, Hitler went too far. Despite warnings from the state police, he decided to break up the May Day parade planned by leftist groups. Then, rumors circulated that outlawed Communist paramilitary units, hidden since the days of the Bavarian Soviet Republic, would defend the leftist march. That suited Hitler perfectly; he would annihilate the Reds,

but he would need army weapons. He and Röhm put in their request—almost a demand—and were astonished when Lossow curtly refused to go along. Röhm then took the brazen step of opening army arms dumps on his own authority. When Lossow learned of this insubordination, he reacted as would any German general officer. Trucks filled with regular troops roared up to the stadium where the SA had received its weapons; the Nazis suddenly found themselves surrounded and stood there in disbelief. Then they returned the arms.

The leftists staged their May Day march without interference. In Munich and elsewhere, the credibility of Hitler and his minions was seriously diminished. Röhm was dismissed from his prestigious staff job for "grave derelictions" and assigned to a rifle company.

The setback was only temporary. By September, as events approached a crescendo, Hitler was ready again. He had previously denounced Berlin for tolerating the French hold on the Ruhr, ridiculing the government's campaign of passive resistance. Now he attacked with equal venom the government's decision to end this resistance. Meanwhile, the mark's value was entering a free-fall stage, and he fulminated against that as well. Hitler's violent rhetoric restored him with his party somewhat. But at a gigantic right-wing rally that drew 200,000 to Nuremberg, ninety miles north of Munich, the Führer was only one among many leaders on the reviewing stand. General Ludendorff, the old war-horse, was the center of attention, gravely taking the marchers' salutes; Hitler seemed to sidle close to the great man.

The tension grew ever higher. Ceasing even passive resistance in the Ruhr struck Germans everywhere as the end of all decency and honor. Furthermore, by now the currency was of virtually no value. A glass of beer at Berlin's Hotel Adlon cost 3.5 million marks; the price of a dinner in the evening would barely cover a cup of coffee the next morning; and people told sour jokes about the thief who came upon a huge basket of bills but left the money in favor of the basket. Talk of revolution was constant. In Saxony and Thuringia, just to the north of Bavaria, Communist paramilitary

Captain Ernst Röhm used his position on the district commander's staff in Munich to supply the Nazis with men, money, and arms. His patronage shielded the party from local authorities after its members started using roughneck tactics.

groups were preparing to impose Red regimes on the people. In Bavaria itself, the fabric of society seemed on the verge of ripping apart, and Minister-President Knilling turned over power to Kahr, naming him general state commissioner—in effect, dictator. Kahr understood immediately that he could rule only with the full support of the police and the army. Kahr, Seisser, and, most importantly, General Lossow, thus formed a ruling triumvirate. In the meantime, Hitler maneuvered to push the trio in the direction he wanted.

September and October were times of peril and opportunity. Various scenarios presented themselves to the Bavarian leaders. The Communist danger to Saxony and Thuringia might offer an opportunity for Bavaria to invade its neighbors in the name of national unity—and then, with the populace on its side, extend the march to Berlin. Another prospect often mentioned in rightist circles was that General Seeckt might be pressured into setting up a national military dictatorship. Kahr had his own agenda: Let Bavaria secede, restore the Wittelsbach throne, and strike an alliance with Austria to the south.

Hitler, on the outside, saw opportunities in an invasion of Saxony and Thuringia, but the other two ideas enraged him. He knew that Seeckt would never mount the sweeping blood purges necessary to cleanse Germany—and besides, he, Hitler, was the only man fit to rule the nation. His reaction was to attack Seeckt in the columns of the *Völkischer Beobachter* for having a Jewish wife and thus by implication being a party to the great Jewish-Marxist conspiracy. In reply, the enraged Seeckt ordered Lossow to shut down the Nazi newspaper. This, however, would have gone down badly with the free-spirited Bavarians, and State Commissioner Kahr ordered Lossow not to touch the paper. The general obeyed. As the dispute between Berlin and Munich escalated, Seeckt relieved Lossow of command—and Kahr thereupon took a momentous step, one that was unprecedented in the history of the German army and flatly treasonous to Berlin. He declared that all troops within Bavaria were Bavarian, not federal, forces; he demanded—and received—

War hero Hermann Göring, who commanded Germany's renowned Flying Circus in 1918 after the death of Manfred von Richthofen, joined Hitler's party in 1922 because "it was the only one with the guts to say, 'to hell with Versailles!'"

an oath of loyalty to the state, and he reinstalled Lossow as commander of the regional Reichswehr. For his own reasons, Hitler supported this egregious disloyalty. Speaking to the officer cadets of the infantry academy, he solemnly told them: "Your highest obligation under your oath to the flag, gentlemen, is to break that oath."

The stage was set for confrontation, and that is exactly what Kahr planned. He summoned the Freikorps' Captain Ehrhardt and invited him to join in a march against the Berlin government, which he scathingly described as a "colossus with feet of clay." Lossow and the Bavarian Reichswehr would participate as well. The operation was code-named Sunrise, and the date was to be November 15. But then, in a swirl of events, the situation changed dramatically. Seeckt sent regular army troops to put down the Marxists in Saxony and Thuringia, and the Berlin government took economic action that showed promise of controlling inflation. All at once the storm clouds parted. Colonel Seisser of the state police visited Berlin and returned in early November with discouraging words for Kahr. This was no time for a putsch.

Hitler faced pressures of his own. All the apocalyptic oratory had whipped his Storm Troopers into a frenzy. Sturmabteilung leaders told him that if he did not move promptly, the SA might march without him, following any leader who might appear. Hitler saw little choice. He summoned his cohorts and announced a coup against the Bavarian government; then all Bavaria would march against Berlin. The date was set for November 11.

It would be a Sunday, the ideal time to strike. The government would be at a standstill; officials would be away; the police and military as relaxed as they ever got. The directive included the phrase "March in with music"—and there would be good reason for martial airs. Sunday, November 11, would be the fifth anniversary of Germany's humiliating 1918 surrender. What better moment to declare a German national revival?

Within a few days, however, Hitler canceled those plans and abruptly chose the evening of November 8. Actually, Gustav Kahr had chosen the new date for him. The state commissioner announced a major meeting to be held in the huge 3,000-seat Bürgerbräukeller, at which he would outline his economic and governmental plans for the future. Hitler was invited to attend, along with a varied group of dignitaries and agitators. Kahr had been cool to Hitler of late, and the suspicion was growing that he was about to proclaim his own putsch from which the Nazis would be excluded—a coup that would separate Bavaria from Berlin, restore the Wittelsbach monarchy, and install Kahr as the leader of the conservative restoration. All of which was totally unacceptable to Hitler. But if he could strike first

Hitler, who never obtained a driver's license, arrives at a 1923 rally in a high-powered Mercedes-Benz. The Mercedes was a modified racing car, and since races in Germany went clockwise, the driver sat on the right to help prevent the car from spinning out.

with a dramatic action that evening, he might swing the people behind him and force Kahr, Lossow, and Seisser onto the Nazi bandwagon. Beyond that, little planning was done. The Nazis would simply capture Kahr's meeting. Once that was accomplished, the Storm Troopers would move on military targets, including army headquarters.

The event started at 8:15 p.m. before a full house in the Bürgerbräukeller. Kahr had been droning on for about twenty minutes—he had, in fact, called the affair to speak about economics—when Hitler drove up in a red Mercedes-Benz. After him came several truckloads of uniformed and heavily armed Storm Troopers. One squad of fifteen men led by Hermann Göring rushed through the lobby, burst open the doors of the hall, and set up a heavy machine gun, its muzzle trained on the audience. The plan was for Hitler to stride to the podium and announce the coup, but the noise of his arrival and of his men setting up machine guns created pandemonium. Immediately, the aisles filled with shouting people, and Hitler found himself struggling through a tide of humanity. Kahr had stopped speaking. Near the podium, Hitler mounted a chair with a pistol in his hand and fired a shot into the ceiling. The crowd fell into shocked silence.

"The national revolution has broken out!" cried Hitler in a raw voice, waving the pistol wildly. He was wearing a cutaway, with his Iron Cross prominently displayed. (One observer, finding him curiously unprepossessing, thought to himself, "That poor little waiter.") Hitler shouted, "The Bavarian government and the Reich government are deposed!" and he added, untruthfully, that the army and state police already had joined the new movement. He jumped off the chair, scrambled over a table, and climbed up onto the podium where Kahr, Lossow, and Seisser were stand-

ing, rigid with fury. "Your Excellency Kahr, Your Excellency Lossow, and Colonel Seisser," said Hitler harshly, "I must respectfully ask you to go with me. I guarantee your safety."

In a small side room, Hitler faced his captives. They stood in silence, glaring, mistrustful, and somehow contemptuous. Colonel Seisser upbraided Hitler for breaking his word not to launch a putsch. "I did it for the good of Germany. Forgive me," said Hitler. He forbade the trio to speak with one another, then explained that he was establishing a new regime in Bavaria that would be the foundation of a new government for the nation. Nervously, pistol in hand, he said, "I have four bullets. Three for you if you fail me, the last for myself."

In the large room, people were growing restless. Catcalls of "Sideshow!" rose from the crowd at the apparent travesty being acted out. As the protest rose to an angry rumble, it was Göring's turn to fire a shot into the ceiling. He climbed onto the podium and bellowed that Kahr and his fellows were in no danger. It would all be clarified soon. "And anyway," he shouted, "you've got your beer. What are you worrying about?"

Presently Hitler returned to the podium. He started to speak and quickly struck his mesmerizing stride. Before long, thundering ovations were audible to the three angry men in the side room. Hitler laid out his new government: He would rule as dictator, Ludendorff would head the army, Lossow the defense ministry, Seisser the national police, while Kahr would lead Bavaria. He intended to coopt these men, not overcome them.

Now the SA troops waiting in various other beer halls could be told: The

Gathering momentum for the November putsch, uniformed Nazis march through the streets of Nuremberg *(below)*. At left, Hitler attends a parade flanked by Alfred Rosenberg *(in wing collar)*, editor of the party newspaper, and Friedrich Weber, leader of a freelance military unit allied to Hitler.

putsch was on. Screaming their delight, they streamed out to arm themselves for the attack. One gang of 400 Storm Troopers approached the Engineer Barracks, where a mere seven soldiers under an officer guarded a mass of weapons. Other Storm Troopers moved on to the 1st Battalion Barracks, and Röhm led a contingent to seize army headquarters in downtown Munich. The officer in charge, a Captain Wilhelm Daser, quickly surrendered and retired to a nearby building. Röhm let him go, since he had been assured that Lossow would soon order the army to join the putsch. Cadets at the officers' training academy needed no urging; avid Hitler supporters, they joyously marched a thousand strong to the Bürgerbräukeller, the first formation of the regular German army to march openly under the flag of the Nazis.

But the triumvirate was not easily cowed. Hitler was becoming frantic, when the legendary Ludendorff arrived with an escort of SA men. The general was highly annoyed because he had not been given advance notice and because Hitler had taken the top role he had anticipated for himself. But he informed the three that they must support the putsch for the good of Germany. Turning to the two officers as soldier to soldier, he growled, "All right, gentlemen, come along with us, and give me your hand on it." Some said that Lossow accepted his former chief's orders with moist eyes and quivering voice. It took a bit longer before Kahr would pledge himself to the putsch, but eventually, he too gave Ludendorff his hand on it.

The men followed the Führer back to the podium, where each publicly agreed to the new order. "Hitler was radiant with a kind of childlike joy," an observer remembered. The putsch had succeeded. Bavaria now, Germany next. With bursting emotion, he recalled the pledge he had made five years earlier "as a blind cripple in the hospital, not to rest until the November Criminals are cast down and until, from the ruins of the wretched Germany of today, a new nation shall arise—a Germany of greatness, freedom, and glory. Amen!" The crowd leaped to its feet, and "Deutschland, Deutschland über Alles" resounded through the hall.

Then word came of a hitch in the plans. At the Engineer Barracks the lone officer and his handful of soldiers had duped the 400 Storm Troopers, locked them inside the drill hall, and covered the exits with machine guns. Hitler hurried off to deal with the problem, leaving Ludendorff with the triumvirate while the audience slowly filed out and went home. On the way, Hitler heard of Röhm's success at army headquarters downtown and went there first. Since he accepted the triumvirate's conversion at face value, he assumed that orders from Lossow would shortly end any military resistance. Neither he nor Röhm knew that Captain Daser, the officer who had retired to a nearby building, had in fact closeted himself in a communi-

The Ehrhardt Brigade, the most feared Freikorps fighters in Germany, await orders on Bavaria's northern border in October 1923. Sworn in as emergency police by Bavarian authorities, the brigade was placed to help counter armed extremists, such as the Nazis, or march on Berlin.

cations room; as the evening developed, Daser would play a key role in putting down the putsch.

Back at the beer hall, the triumvirate suggested to Ludendorff that the hour was late and that it was time to go home. The general agreed, and the three men upon whose cooperation the putsch depended vanished into the night. When Hitler protested their disappearance, Ludendorff sternly forbade him to doubt the word of a German officer.

Lossow went immediately to his Munich district headquarters. There a subordinate asked pointedly, "Excellency, surely that was all bluff?" The message was clear; his officers would not support the putsch. And they

soon had backing from Berlin. News of the events in Munich had reached the capital at about half past eleven that night. At an emergency cabinet meeting, President Ebert faced General Seeckt and asked the critical question. "Tell us, please," he inquired, "whom does the Reichswehr obey, the government or the mutineers?" Seeckt coolly cast his monocled gaze around the table. "Herr Reich President," he said, "the army obeys me."

Returning to his headquarters, Seeckt telegraphed Lossow in Munich to suppress the uprising at once—or he, Seeckt, would see to it himself, with everything that would entail. If Lossow had any remaining doubts about his course, they had just been resolved. His officers contacted Daser in the downtown communications center, and Daser was soon relaying orders to units from afar to smash the Nazi coup. Before long, Kahr arrived to join Lossow, while Seisser was in his own headquarters lining up police battalions against the putsch.

All the while, Hitler's Storm Troopers were demonstrating what life would be like under the Nazis. They announced peoples' courts to judge enemies of the state; death without appeal was the sole sentence for a verdict of guilty. Then they set out to find victims for these courts, beating and arresting Jews and Socialists in the streets, wrecking opposition-newspaper plants, burning papers as they one day would burn books.

It was hours before the Nazis realized that the situation had turned against them. Later, Hitler was faulted for not having seized key telegraph and telephone and railway centers. He had made no such plans because he was confident that, with a little prodding, the authorities would swiftly swing into line. Throughout the long night this delusion held, long after the triumvirate's silence should have told him otherwise. Gradually, the truth began to dawn as he sat with Ludendorff among his hungry SA men in the beer hall. At downtown army headquarters, Röhm found himself surrounded by a cordon of regulars, a cannon drawn up, machine guns mounted on roofs commanding his positions. The Storm Troopers were former soldiers, and the army did not want to fire on them. Then one of Röhm's men nervously let go a shot. Instantly the machine guns opened fire. Two putschists were killed. The first blood had been drawn.

At the Bürgerbräukeller, Hitler was in a funk, virtually incapacitated. By morning, it was clear that the putsch was failing. Reports told of Reichswehr troops putting down pro-Hitler uprisings in Augsburg, Nuremberg, and Regensburg. Fresh army units were moving into Munich with armored cars and mortars to control key squares. State police were occupying bridges across the Isar River, which bisected the city.

Göring suggested that they retreat to his strongly pro-Nazi hometown of Rosenheim on the Austrian border; there they could regroup and await

Off-duty soldiers idle at the arched entrance to the Bürgerbräukeller, which remained a popular beer hall while becoming a Nazi shrine as the site of the 1923 putsch. The Nazis considered the place a perfect cover: As one of them said, "No one will suspect a man with his nose in a stein of beer."

better circumstances. But Ludendorff would have none of it. "We'll march!" he barked. Hitler said that the army or police might fire. Ludendorff glared. Fire on the old commander? Impossible. "We'll march!"

Later Hitler said that the idea was to present themselves to the populace, or, as he put it, "to go into the city to win the people to our side." The march got under way at about noon, and in fact, enthusiastic crowds did line the streets, cheering and waving swastika flags as the Nazis passed by. They met their first opposition when they reached the east side of the Isar River, where a unit of Colonel Seisser's state police had lined up to stop them. Ludendorff led the way, Hitler just behind him with Göring. As they approached the police, someone shouted, "Don't fire, Ludendorff is with us." The police lowered their rifles and were seized by the Nazis. It looked easy.

When the marchers reached a central plaza, they milled around, not knowing where to go next. Again it was Ludendorff who settled matters. He turned toward the army headquarters where Röhm was trapped. He intended to rescue his men.

The marchers turned with him onto a narrower street, at the head of which another group of police waited. An army veteran among the Nazis saw that these men were prepared for action. As the column approached, there were more cries announcing Ludendorff, but this time to no avail. The police moved forward with rifles across their chests in classic crowd-control formation. The two sides closed. Then it happened. A police lieu-

tenant recalled: "Suddenly, a Hitler man who stood one half step left of me fired a pistol at my head. The shot went by me and killed Sergeant Hollweg behind me. Before I could give an order, my people opened fire."

Answering fire crashed from the Nazi ranks. Hitler had linked arms with a man beside him who was killed instantly, pulling down the Führer as he fell. Göring was critically wounded in the groin. A machine gun in a police scout car opened sweeping fire. The Nazis, being experienced soldiers, went prone, answering with rifle fire. The exchange went on for at least thirty seconds, an eternity in such a situation. A Nazi remembered: "Everywhere people were going down, writhing on the ground in agony, dead and dying, while the guns still rattled into their stampeding midst. Dead were trampled under people's feet, throwing the living down; blood flowed everywhere over the gray pavement. Shrieks and cries rent the air, and always that insane firing went on."

Then it was over. In the sudden silence, the cries of the wounded began to be heard. A surprised observer realized all at once that everyone who could had fled. Fourteen Nazis were dead or dying. The number of wounded was never counted since the beaten rebels melted away, hiding their weapons and ripping off swastika armbands. Three police officers had been killed, and others were wounded.

General Ludendorff, by most accounts, dropped to the ground when the firing started; now he stood unhurt and marched straight on into the police lines and presented himself for arrest. Hitler, in great pain from a dislocated shoulder though untouched by the firing, made an ignominious picture. He was the first to stand up when the shooting stopped, but without looking at his troops he ran to the rear. There, someone pushed him into an automobile, a yellow Opel that raced away.

Two days later, Hitler was arrested. He felt that his life was over, his leadership destroyed. But he rallied in the weeks before his trial for treason, and when he came before a sympathetic court, he turned defeat into a demagogic triumph that spread his name across Germany—indeed, the world. Readily admitting his putsch, he justified it in furious, mesmerizing speeches that began as answers to prosecutors' questions and ran on for hours, propounding those views that found such resonance in a desperate Germany. He later referred to the setback of November 9, 1923, as "perhaps the greatest stroke of luck of my life." And he could say, "Before the march, I had 70,000 or 80,000 followers. After the march, I had 2,000,000." He spent a pro forma nine months in prison, where he was treated as an honored guest and visited by dignitaries. There he dictated *Mein Kampf*, the testament that would make him a millionaire, and plotted his route to power.

Within a decade he would triumph. ✚

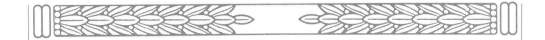

Defendants Erich Ludendorff (*left*), Hitler, and Friedrich Weber huddle during a pause in the 1924 "trial of the age." Ludendorff was acquitted; Weber and Hitler were sentenced to five years. After nine months, Hitler was released and began to rebuild his movement.

A Premature Push for Power

"What kind of revolution do you call this?" groused Paul Goebel, one of the uniformed thugs trucked into Munich early on November 9, 1923, to support Adolf Hitler's grab for power. Like his fellow Storm Troopers, Goebel thought the state police and local army units would join the revolt, but as his truck rumbled over the empty, stone-paved streets, he was no longer certain. "Something's wrong," he muttered.

The putsch had started well enough the night before. Heavily armed Nazis had stormed the Bürgerbräukeller, where they seized the three most powerful officials in Bavaria and proclaimed a new national government, to be led by Hitler and General Erich Ludendorff, the renowned war hero. But after the three mouthed support for the new regime, Ludendorff trustingly set them free, and by doing so threw the putsch into confusion: Would the trio support the rebellion or crush it?

In the morning, both Hitler and the government took their appeals directly to the people. While Storm Troopers hurried up and down Munich's medieval streets, hanging posters that proclaimed the revolution (inset), police patrols tramped from kiosk to kiosk, slapping up their own freshly printed placards that condemned the putsch as high treason. Hitler's troops arrested policemen while the police arrested SA men, and each side tore down the other's posters. Later, citizens on their way to work stood befuddled in the damp autumn air before billboards and newsstands on which opposing posters hung side by side.

Nonetheless, many Müncheners remained unaware of the rift between the government and the putschists. Inflamed by Nazi firebrands, conservative burghers joined ranks with Hitler's armed Freebooters as they marched behind red, white, and black swastika banners from the Bürgerbräukeller to the heart of Munich. There, however, the police and regular army put an emphatic end to confusion with a flurry of gunfire, bloodily putting down the putsch and elevating Adolf Hitler to international celebrity.

Equipped with swastika armbands, backpacks, and rifles, helmeted soldiers of Shock Troop Adolf Hitler climb down from the beer truck that carried them to Munich. Hours earlier, Hitler had distributed posters *(inset)* to herald his new revolutionary government.

Proklamation
an das deutsche Volk!

Die Regierung der November-verbrecher in Berlin ist heute für abgesetzt erklärt worden.

Eine provisorische deutsche National-Regierung ist gebildet worden.

Diese besteht aus

General Ludendorff, Adolf Hitler
General von Lossow, Oberst von Seisser

In a wet snowfall, Hitler's forces
march from the Bürgerbräukeller
to the city center. The Nazi leader
hoped an outpouring of support
by civilians lining the route would
persuade the army not to shoot,
but he forbade his men to bring
along a hostage, Eduard Schmid,
Munich's Socialist mayor *(inset,
wearing topcoat)*. "I don't want
any martyrs," he snapped.

Standing on the seat of an open car, one of the Nazis' most scurrilous orators, Julius Streicher, rouses a crowd in front of Munich's city hall. Unaware that the authorities were placing troops and armor around the city, the citizens cheered Streicher and lustily sang the national anthem when he finished speaking.

After repulsing the rebels with gunfire, mounted Bavarian state police with lances at the ready sweep across the Odeonsplatz to clear it of any remaining Nazis. Their actions stunned Ludendorff, who had expected the police and army to follow him always. "The heavens will fall," he had said, "before the Bavarian Reichswehr turns against me!"

An armored truck drawn up in front of the Sendlingertor, a 600-year-old city gate, evokes wary glances from passersby after the putsch. Despite such efforts by the Reichswehr to intercept fleeing Nazis, Hitler eluded immediate capture and found refuge in a country house thirty-five miles south of Munich.

Acknowledgments and Picture Credits

The editors thank: England: London—Terry Charman, Paul Kemp, Allan Williams, Michael Willis, Imperial War Museum. Telford—Simon Taylor, The Weimar Archive. Federal Republic of Germany: Berlin— Diethart Kerbs, ABC Archiv; Heidi Klein, Bildarchiv Preussischer Kulturbesitz; Gabrielle Kohler, Jürgen Raible, Archiv für Kunst und Geschichte; Wolfgang Schäche; Wolfgang Streubel, Ullstein Bilderdienst. Koblenz—Meinrad Nilges, Bundesarchiv; Klaus Weschenfelder, Mittelrhein-Museum. Munich—Elisabeth Heidt, Süddeutscher Verlag Bilderdienst; Robert Hoffmann; Claus Offermann; Michael Stephan, Bayerisches Hauptstaatsarchiv. France: Bayeux—Georges and Rozenn Bernage, Editions Heimdal. German Democratic Republic: Berlin—René Grohnert, Museum für Deutsche Geschichte; Hannes Quaschinsky, ADN-Zentralbild. Italy: Florence—Emanuela Sesti, Archivio Alinari; Imelda Siviero. United States: District of Columbia—Elizabeth Hill, Jim Trimble, National Archives; Eveline Nave, Library of Congress; George Snowden, Snowden Associates. New Jersey—Al Collett. Virginia—George A. Petersen, National Capital Historical Sales.

Credits from left to right are separated by semicolons, from top to bottom by dashes. Cover: Presseillustrationen Heinrich R. Hoffmann, Munich. 4, 5: Archiv für Kunst und Geschichte, West Berlin. 6: Roger-Viollet, Paris. 9: Archiv für Kunst und Geschichte, West Berlin. 11: National Gallery, London. 12, 13: Map by R. R. Donnelley and Sons Company, Cartographic Services. 14: Archiv für Kunst und Geschichte, West Berlin. 15: From *Wilhelm II* by J. A. De Jonge, De Bataafsche Leeuw, 1986. 18, 19: From *Das Eiserne Kreuz*, Verlag der Eiserne Hammer, Leipzig (2); Historia-Photo, Hamburg, from *The New Encyclopædia Britannica* (Vol. 5), Chicago, 1974—from *Das Eiserne Kreuz*, Verlag der Eiserne Hammer, Leipzig. 21: Weimar Archive, Telford. 22: Camera Press, London. 26, 27: FPG International, N.Y.—H. Guttmann from Black Star, N.Y. 28, 29: Archiv für Kunst und Geschichte, West Berlin. 31: Map by R. R. Donnelley and Sons Company, Cartographic Services. 32: The Granger Collection, N.Y.; Bildarchiv Preussischer Kulturbesitz (BPK), West Berlin—The Granger Collection, N.Y. 33: Globe Photos, N.Y.; The Granger Collection, N.Y.—The Granger Collection, N.Y.; Globe Photos, N.Y. 34, 35: Camera Press, London; from *Bismarck im Sachsenwald* by Arthur Rehbein, Buchverlag der Gesellschaft zur Verbreitung Klassischer Kunst, Berlin, 1925. 36-39: Larry Sherer, courtesy Gary Gerber, except background

Larry Sherer, courtesy Kirk Denkler. 40, 41: BPK, West Berlin. 42, 43: Bundesarchiv, Koblenz; Photoreporters, Inc., N.Y. 44, 45: Copied by Larry Sherer, from *Dokumente zur Geschichte der Arbeiterbewegung in Württemberg und Baden 1848-1949*, selected and compiled by Peter Scherer and Peter Schaaf, Konrad Theiss Verlag, Stuttgart, 1984, Historia-Photo, Hamburg. 46, 47: Courtesy Editions Heimdal, Bayeux, France; Imperial War Museum, London. 48: Bundesarchiv, Koblenz—BPK, West Berlin. 49: Courtesy Editions Heimdal, Bayeux, France. 50, 51: Hulton Deutsch Collection, London. 52, 53: National Archives no. 11-SC-94980; Imperial War Museum, London. 54, 55: Imperial War Museum, London (2)—from *Wir Kämpfer im Weltkrieg*, Neufeld & Henius, Berlin, 1979. 56, 57: Imperial War Museum, London; BPK, West Berlin. 58: Popperfoto, London. 61: Bundesarchiv, Koblenz; Culver Pictures, N.Y. 62: Ullstein Bilderdienst, West Berlin— Presseillustrationen Heinrich R. Hoffmann, Munich. 63: Ullstein Bilderdienst, West Berlin—Bundesarchiv, Koblenz; Archives Tallandier, Paris. 64, 65: Presseillustrationen Heinrich R. Hoffmann, Munich. 66, 67: Performing Arts Research Center, New York Public Library. 68: From *Adolf Hitler, Mein Jugendfreund* by August Kubizek, Leopold Stöcker, Graz und Göttingen, 1953. 70: Popperfoto, London—from *Adolf Hitler, Mein Jugendfreund* by August Kubizek, Leopold Stöcker, Graz und Göttingen, 1953. 71: Popperfoto, London—Presseillustrationen Heinrich R. Hoffmann, Munich. 74, 75: Library of Congress. 76: © Franz Hubmann, Austria. 77: © Franz Hubmann, Austria; BPK, West Berlin—© Franz Hubmann, Austria. 79: Library of Congress. 82-85: Presseillustrationen Heinrich R. Hoffmann, Munich. 87: Presseillustrationen Heinrich R. Hoffmann, Munich. 88: Bundesarchiv, Koblenz (2)—from *Adolf Hitler, Mein Jugendfreund* by August Kubizek, Leopold Stöcker, Graz und Göttingen, 1953 (2). 89: Reproduced by permission of the Marquess of Bath, Longleat House, Warminster, Wiltshire, Great Britain. 90, 91: Reproduced by permission of the Marquess of Bath, Longleat House, Warminster, Wiltshire, Great Britain—Archivio Alinari, Florence, courtesy Professor Rodolfo Siviero's heir, Florence (3). 92, 93: BPK, West Berlin (2); Bayerisches Hauptstaatsarchiv, Munich; Presseillustrationen Heinrich R. Hoffmann, Munich—courtesy U.S. Army, Center of Military History. 94: Archiv Zeitgeschichte Gräfer, Berlin. 97: BPK, West Berlin. 98, 99: Bundesarchiv, Koblenz; Photoreporters, Inc., N.Y. 101: Ullstein Bilderdienst, West Berlin.

102, 103: ABZ, Berlin. 106: Ullstein Bilderdienst, West Berlin. 107: ABZ, Berlin. 108: Ullstein Bilderdienst, West Berlin. 109: Archiv für Kunst und Geschichte, West Berlin. 111: Map by R. R. Donnelley and Sons Company, Cartographic Services. 112, 113: National Archives. 115: Edimedia, Paris—Ullstein Bilderdienst, West Berlin. 117: Archiv für Kunst und Geschichte, West Berlin. 118, 119: Bundesarchiv, Koblenz; Ullstein Bilderdienst, West Berlin. 121: Terry Goodapple/Weinand Militaria—Ullstein Bilderdienst, West Berlin. 122, 123: Ullstein Bilderdienst, West Berlin. 125: BPK, West Berlin—The Granger Collection, N.Y. 126: Library of Congress no. LC 5956—Ullstein Bilderdienst, West Berlin. 127: Ullstein Bilderdienst, West Berlin. 128, 129: The Granger Collection, N.Y.—Deutsche Bundesbank Geldmuseum, Frankfurt. 131: ABZ, Berlin. 132, 133: Süddeutscher Verlag Bilderdienst, Munich—from *Illustrierte Geschichte der deutschen November Revolution 1918/1919*, Dietz, Berlin, 1978, courtesy Museum für Deutsche Geschichte, Berlin GDR. 134, 135: Willy Römer/ABZ, Berlin. 136, 137: Culver Pictures, N.Y. 138, 139: From *Illustrierte Geschichte der deutschen November Revolution 1918/1919*, Dietz, Berlin, 1978, courtesy Museum für Deutsche Geschichte, Berlin GDR; Ullstein Bilderdienst, West Berlin. 140, 141: Pathé News; Willy Römer/ABZ, Berlin. 142, 143: Willy Römer/ABZ, Berlin. 144: Edimedia, Paris. 146, 147: Presseillustrationen Heinrich R. Hoffmann, Munich. 149: Ullstein Bilderdienst, West Berlin—Süddeutscher Verlag Bilderdienst, Munich. 150, 151: Süddeutscher Verlag Bilderdienst, Munich— Edimedia, Paris; Presseillustrationen Heinrich R. Hoffmann, Munich. 152: Bundesarchiv, Koblenz; Süddeutscher Verlag Bilderdienst, Munich. 153: Presseillustrationen Heinrich R. Hoffmann, Munich. 154, 155: Courtesy U.S. Army, Center of Military History. 159: Vorderasiatisches Museum, Staatliche Museen zu Berlin GDR; Mike and Mark Chenault, Albert Speer Archive, Dallas. 160: Ullstein Bilderdienst, West Berlin. 162, 163: Library of Congress no. LC 30544. 164: Foto Heinrich R. Hoffmann, BPK, West Berlin. 165: Süddeutscher Verlag Bilderdienst, Munich. 167: Library of Congress no. LC 4589. 168, 169: BPK, West Berlin; Bundesarchiv, Koblenz. 170, 171: Roger-Viollet, Paris. 173: National Archives. 175: Süddeutscher Verlag Bilderdienst, Munich. 176, 177: Ullstein Bilderdienst, West Berlin; inset, Presseillustrationen Heinrich R. Hoffmann, Munich. 178, 179: Ullstein Bilderdienst, West Berlin. 180, 181: Library of Congress no. LC 30551. 182, 183: Bundesarchiv, Koblenz. 184, 185: Roger-Viollet, Paris.

Bibliography

Books

Balfour, Michael, *The Kaiser and His Times*. New York: W. W. Norton, 1972.

Barnett, Correlli, *The Swordbearers*. London: Eyre & Spottiswoode, 1963.

Binding, Rudolf, *A Fatalist at War*. Transl. by Ian F. D. Morrow. Boston: Houghton Mifflin, 1929.

Buffetaut, Yves, *Mars-Juin 1918: Échec à Ludendorff*. Bayeux, France: Editions Heimdal, 1988.

Bullock, Alan, *Hitler: A Study in Tyranny*. New York: Harper & Row, 1964.

Childs, David, *Germany since 1918*. New York: Harper & Row, 1971.

Cowley, Robert, *1918: Gamble for Victory*. New York: Macmillan, 1964.

Craig, Gordon A.:
Germany 1866-1945. New York: Oxford University Press, 1978.
The Politics of the Prussian Army 1640-1945. London: Oxford University Press, 1955.

Davidson, Eugene, *The Making of Adolf Hitler*. New York: Macmillan, 1977.

De Jonge, Alex, *The Weimar Chronicle*. New York: Paddington Press, 1978.

Dornberg, John, *Munich 1923: The Story of Hitler's First Grab for Power*. New York: Harper & Row, 1982.

Everett, Susanne, *Lost Berlin*. Greenwich, Ct.: Bison Books, 1979.

Eyck, Erich:
A History of the Weimar Republic. Transl. by Harlan P. Hanson and Robert G. L. Waite. Cambridge, Mass.: Harvard University Press, 1967.

Fest, Joachim C., *Hitler*. Transl. by Richard and Clara Winston. New York: Vintage Books, 1975.

Flood, Charles Bracelen, *Hitler: The Path to Power*. Boston: Houghton Mifflin, 1989.

Gies, Joseph, *Crisis 1918*. New York: W. W. Norton, 1974.

Gordon, Harold J., Jr., *The Reichswehr and the German Republic 1919-1926*. Princeton, N.J.: Princeton University Press, 1957.

Grunberger, Richard, *Red Rising in Bavaria*. London: Arthur Barker, 1973.

Grunfeld, Frederic V., *The Hitler File*. New York: Random House, 1974.

Halperin, S. William, *Germany Tried Democracy: A Political History of the Reich from 1918 to 1933*. New York: W. W. Norton, 1965.

Hanser, Richard, *Putsch! How Hitler Made Revolution*. New York: Peter H. Wyden, 1970.

Hausner, Hans Erik, ed., *Das historische Nachrichten-Magazin: 1923*. Vienna: Verlag Carl Ueberreuter, 1982.

Heiden, Konrad, *Der Fuehrer: Hitler's Rise to Power*. Transl. by Ralph Manheim.

Boston: Houghton Mifflin, 1944.

Hitler, Adolf, *Mein Kampf*. Transl. by Ralph Manheim. Boston: Houghton Mifflin, 1971.

Hoffmann, Heinrich, ed., *Hitler wie ihn keiner kennt*. Munich: Verlag Heinrich Hoffmann, 1938.

Hoffmann, Herbert, *Berlin vor fünfzig Jahren*. Berlin: Rembrandt Verlag, 1978.

Holborn, Hajo, *A History of Modern Germany 1840-1945*. New York: Alfred A. Knopf, 1969.

Jenks, William A., *Vienna and the Young Hitler*. New York: Columbia University Press, 1960.

Jetzinger, Franz, *Hitler's Youth*. Transl. by Lawrence Wilson. London: Hutchinson, 1958.

Jones, Nigel H., *Hitler's Heralds: The Story of the Freikorps 1918-1923*. London: John Murray, 1987.

Judd, Denis, *Posters of World War Two*. New York: St. Martin's Press, 1973.

Kehr, Helen, and Janet Langmaid, eds., *The Nazi Era 1919-1945*. London: Mansell Publishing, 1982.

Kerbs, Diethart, ed., *Willy Römer: Januarkämpfe Berlin 1919*. Berlin: Dirk Nishen Verlag in Kreuzberg, 1984.

Kohn, Hans, *The Mind of Germany*. New York: Charles Scribner's Sons, 1960.

Kubizek, August, *The Young Hitler I Knew*. Transl. by E. V. Anderson. Boston: Houghton Mifflin, 1955.

Legge, Edward, *The Public and Private Life of Kaiser William II*. London: Eveleigh Nash, 1915.

Ludwig, Emil, *Bismarck: The Story of a Fighter*. Transl. by Eden and Cedar Paul. Boston: Little, Brown, 1928.

Martin Greenwald Associates, *Historical Maps on File*. New York: Facts On File Publications, 1984.

Middlebrook, Martin, *The Kaiser's Battle*. London: Allen Lane, 1978.

Morgan, J. H., *Assize of Arms*. New York: Oxford University Press, 1946.

Mosse, George L., *The Crisis of German Ideology*. New York: Grosset & Dunlap, 1964.

Nelson, Walter Henry, *The Soldier Kings: The House of Hohenzollern*. New York: G. P. Putnam's Sons, 1970.

Nicholls, A. J., *Weimar and the Rise of Hitler*. London: Macmillan, 1968.

Orlow, Dietrich, *The History of the Nazi Party: 1919-1933*. Pittsburgh: University of Pittsburgh Press, 1969.

Palmer, Alan, *Bismarck*. New York: Charles Scribner's Sons, 1976.

Payne, Robert, *The Life and Death of Adolf Hitler*. New York: Praeger Publishers, 1973.

Picker, Henry, and Heinrich Hoffman, *Hitler Close-Up*. Transl. by Nicholas Fry.

New York: Macmillan, 1973.

Pinson, Koppel S., *Modern Germany*. New York: Macmillan, 1966.

Pitt, Barrie, *1918: The Last Act*. New York: W. W. Norton, 1963.

Röhl, J. C. G., *From Bismarck to Hitler*. London: Longman, 1970.

Rose, Jonathan E., *Otto von Bismarck*. New York: Chelsea House Publishers, 1987.

Scheidemann, Philipp, *The Making of New Germany* (Vol. 2). Transl. by J. E. Michell. New York: D. Appleton, 1929.

Schrader, Bärbel, and Jürgen Schebera, *Kunst-Metropole Berlin 1918-1933*. Berlin, E. Ger.: Aufbau-Verlag Berlin und Weimar, 1987.

Sherman, Franklin, ed., *The Christian in Society* (Vol. 47 of *Luther's Works*). Philadelphia: Fortress Press, 1971.

Shermer, David, *World War I*. London: Derbibooks, 1973.

Smith, Bradley F., *Adolf Hitler*. Stanford, Calif.: Hoover Institution on War, Revolution and Peace, 1967.

Swearingen, Ben E., *The Mystery of Hermann Goering's Suicide*. San Diego: Harcourt Brace Jovanovich, 1985.

Taylor, A. J. P., ed., *History of World War I*. London: Octopus Books, 1974.

Toland, John:
Hitler: The Pictorial Documentary of His Life. Garden City, N.Y.: Doubleday, 1978.

Van der Kiste, John, *Queen Victoria's Children*. Gloucester, England: Alan Sutton, 1986.

Viereck, Peter, *Metapolitics: The Roots of the Nazi Mind*. New York: Capricorn Books, 1961.

Waite, Robert G. L.:
The Psychopathic God: Adolf Hitler. New York: Basic Books, 1977.
Vanguard of Nazism. Cambridge, Mass.: Harvard University Press, 1952.

Waldersee, Alfred von, *A Field-Marshal's Memoirs*. Transl. by Frederic Whyte. London: Hutchinson, 1924.

Waldman, Eric, *The Spartacist Uprising of 1919*. Milwaukee: Marquette University Press, 1958.

Walther, Herbert, ed., *Hitler*. New York: Exeter Books, 1984.

Watt, Richard M., *The Kings Depart*. New York: Simon and Schuster, 1968.

Wheeler-Bennett, John W., *The Nemesis of Power*. London: Macmillan, 1964.

Zweig, Stefan, *The World of Yesterday*. Lincoln, Nebr.: University of Nebraska Press, 1964.

Other Publications

Freed, Stanley A., and Ruth S. Freed, "Origin of the Swastika." *Natural History*, January 1980.

Index

Time-Life Books Inc. offers a wide range of fine recordings, including a *Rock 'n' Roll Era* series. For subscription information, call 1-800-621-7026 or write Time-Life Music, P.O. Box C-32068, Richmond, Virginia 23261-2068.